COLLAPSE

ABOUT THE AUTHOR

Ian Kearns is co-founder, former director and board member of the European Leadership Network, a pan-European group of senior political, military and diplomatic leaders drawn from across the continent. He is also a former specialist adviser to the Joint House of Commons/House of Lords Committee on National Security Strategy. Between 2007 and 2009 Ian served as deputy chair and director of secretariat to former NATO secretary general George Robertson and former high representative to Bosnia Paddy Ashdown on the IPPR Commission on National Security Strategy in the 21st Century. His other publications include *Influencing Tomorrow: Future Challenges for British Foreign Policy*, co-edited with Douglas Alexander. Ian has published widely on European and international security issues and has been frequently quoted in the national and international media. He has written for the *Daily Telegraph*, *Prospect* magazine, the *New Statesman*, *The Independent* and

Newsweek. Most recently, he took part in the BBC 2 documentary *World War Three: Inside the War Room*. He lives in London.

INTRODUCTION

This book is a warning, not a prediction. A warning to those who believe the European Union (EU) is out of crisis and to Euro-optimists already busy dreaming of its brighter future. A warning to those who know too little of their own continent's history and who labour under the comfortable but deluded impression that Europe has escaped its past. A warning, above all, to friends of the EU everywhere not to breathe a sigh of relief too soon.

The year 2017 brought good news. The eurozone returned to growth. Emmanuel Macron campaigned on a pro-European platform, and won. Eurosceptic populists flirted with victory in the Netherlands before snatching defeat from its jaws. Chancellor Merkel survived, though only just. And Brexit did not usher in a period of wider Eurosceptic political contagion. But look a little longer, and dig a little deeper, and it is hard to escape a sense of foreboding. Some seem to want to ignore it, and will perhaps view this book as an exercise in scaremongering or in doing the EU down, but that is not the motivation for writing it. To its author, it is a deeply felt gesture of concern for an indispensable European integration project. A project that has delivered the best seven decades of peace and progress in European history and that many in politics across the continent today seem to want to destroy. A project that our forebears embraced in the aftermath of the searing first half of the twentieth century and that embodies, however imperfectly, many of the lessons they learned from that experience. The EU, it has always seemed to me, is a gift from one generation of Europeans to another and a signpost we ignore at our peril. The message it contains could not be clearer: the path to a better life runs through European unity. To head in the other direction is to flirt with hell.

Writing a book like this, about the problems and vulner-abilities facing the European Union today, is therefore not an act of Euroscepticism but a call to action. My case is that the continued existence of the EU is far from secure and that were it to collapse, this would not usher in the bright future of Eurosceptic dreams but would rather open the door instead to an economic, political and geopolitical nightmare: a nightmare that would make the financial crisis of 2007–08 and its aftermath look like a footnote in Europe's annual accounts. The arrogance and complacency with which some members of Europe's governing elite seem to dismiss such a prospect ought to comfort no one. Many of these politicians are the ones who didn't see the last crisis coming and who catastrophically mismanaged it when it did. Their collective judgement deserves no deference. The real danger to Europe comes not from those warning of the danger that still lies ahead but from those who believe the danger has passed. If this book is even half right, the fate of the continent hangs not only in the balance, but by a thread.

This is because the problems facing the European Union today are formidable and structural. From the outside, the institution is more challenged now than it has been for decades. Where once it was thought the institutions of the West would roll eastward, in the post-Cold War world it now seems that the flow is the other way around. Russia is penetrating and destabilising the European Union from the east and China's footprint in Europe is growing. In the south, instability in the Middle East and its spill-over to Europe is dividing Europeans and destroying their internal cohesion. And from the west, the waning of American commitment to Europe, stark in the age of Trump but part of a long-term historical trend towards US withdrawal from the continent, leaves the EU strategically vulnerable and largely unable to act in its own defence.

Internally, the eurozone crisis and its aftermath have destroyed not only much trust in mainstream European political leaders but much solidarity between European peoples.

What was essentially the legally sanctioned heist of the European taxpayer to bail out the banks and in some cases the governments that were too closely associated with them has caused massive economic, social and political damage. The rise of Eurosceptic populism has been but one result. Another has been a change of political atmosphere to one more illiberal than liberal in most EU member states. Populism has, moreover, drawn sustenance from and helped to amplify the glaring lack of solidarity that member states have demonstrated with each other as the European crisis has unfolded. Bail-outs of debtor countries have become politically poisonous both in the countries providing the money and in those receiving it. The lack of agreement on how to handle the flow of migrants and refugees to Europe has made the EU look incompetent and incapable. And both the legitimacy and effectiveness of the European Union have become more widely questioned than ever before as a result.

None of these problems or challenges are going away any time soon. There is more than a strong possibility that all will remain with us at the time of the next European recession. If they do, my view is that the European Union is in such a fragile state that developments will quickly place its continued existence in question. And even before then, and without a new economic downturn, a populist breakthrough could still cause chaos and a new spiral of crisis. It is worth reflecting, as I do in later chapters of this book, on a few of the inconvenient truths of 2017 that act as notes of caution to Euro-optimism. Emmanuel Macron's La République En Marche! won a big victory in the final round of the French parliamentary elections, but it did so on a turnout of less than 50 per cent and with the support of only 25 per cent of the electorate. In Italy, the populist Five Star Movement and Northern League, both deeply Eurosceptic, consistently polled strongly. In Austria, the far-right Freedom Party moved into government. Although Chancellor Merkel just about won the German election, the far-right Alternative für Deutschland (AfD) made a historic breakthrough and now has large representation in the Bundestag. Where the Eurosceptic parties didn't win, as in the Netherlands, they still shaped both the tone and content of the national debate. Just a few years ago such levels of both support and influence for Eurosceptic parties would have been unthinkable. Today, they should be seen for what they are: the representation of a European body politic in deep crisis and of a European electorate pensively on the look-out for something new.

In making my case in the pages that follow, I have not attempted to write an academic book or to mimic an academic style. The issues handled are all the subject of serious and sober study in the academic literature and so they should be. But as a former academic who has spent much of the last twenty years working in think-tanks, politics, business and the media, I have tried to do something a little different. I have written an unashamedly personal, and admittedly subjective, account of what I think is going on in Europe today, and of what is at stake for all of us if it goes wrong. I have not tried to balance or even to qualify every view expressed with counter-arguments to be found elsewhere in the literature. Part of the reason for this is that I have spent much of the last six years of my life co-founding and running a small non-governmental organisation, the European Leadership Network, an experience that has afforded me the chance to talk about European politics, economics and security with some of the continent's pre-eminent statesmen and women, among them many former Prime Ministers, cabinet ministers, military leaders and senior diplomats drawn from across the greater European space. It is from that personal vantage point, and on the basis of the reflections it has stimulated, that I write. If the book's style disappoints my many academic friends, and if my language at times appears unequivocal where in an academic context equivocation might be wise, this acknowledgement of difference will have to suffice as absolution.

The book is divided into three parts. Part 1 outlines the contours of what must be seen as the EU's multidimensional crisis. The challenges to the European project from outside and from within are covered, as are what I consider to be the largely ineffectual responses offered to both so far. Some of the deep divisions within the European Union, and some of the forces out to destroy it, are exposed. Much of this material is the stuff of daily news reports and will come as no surprise to the informed observer. What I do here is try to bring the picture together in its totality in an attempt to locate individual challenges and events in their wider terrain and to connect them together on a larger canvas. Too many people think about Europe from the perspective of this or that policy silo. The point to understand is that the different elements of the European Union's crisis interact with and feed off each other.

Part 2 moves the book into territory that few others have covered in a sustained way by asking what future trigger events could see the European Union tip from its current fragile state into one of collapse. It also explores what Europe after the European Union might look like if it does. Most of the existing studies addressing these questions have grown out of finance houses concerned, back in 2010–12, that the single currency might collapse. They have therefore focused predominantly on what the dynamics of the euro's unravelling might be and on what the overall economic consequences of such an unravelling might look like. Far less attention has been paid to the political and geopolitical consequences that might result. Perhaps the lack of a more extensive literature rests on the belief that collapse is so unlikely or that if it does occur, it would be such a seismic event as to render speculation on what might follow useless. Whatever the reason, this book tries to fill the gap. My argument is that a collapse is not so unlikely and that by being clearer about just how bad the consequences would be, perhaps we might steel ourselves to do more to prevent it.

The book explains what the economic unravelling of the eurozone would look like in practice. It posits a boost to the politics of illiberalism and Euroscepticism in almost any collapse scenario, and it addresses what the end of the European Union would mean for the geopolitics and international relations of the continent. It is in this part of the book that the idea that Europe has escaped its catastrophic past is put most severely to the test. Without the binding that the European Union represents, an already complicated picture would become fiendishly difficult to manage. Without the EU, it is hard to see how Europe avoids a return to the balance-of-power system that so troubled its nineteenth- and twentieth-century past. While some of the actors and alliances may be different, many of the tensions that the EU has so successfully repressed would resurface. And while the rest of the twenty-first century marches on beyond Europe's shores, Europe would be forced to look inward in search of solutions to challenges that faced, and ultimately overwhelmed, previous generations.

Part 3 concludes the book with some thoughts on what needs to happen to avoid the worst. It is not a detailed manifesto. There are already many of these around and most of them strike me as politically implausible. Instead, it is an account of the dynamics that need to be changed if the European Union is to be saved and the ideals that must be fought for if the Union is to command its citizens' loyalty. One of the sources of most profound concern in the current debate is the multitude of routes to possible EU collapse that now exist alongside few plausible reforms that look capable of fending it off. Possible reform initiatives are touched on, but if, like the author, you want the European Union to succeed, it is hard to feel optimistic. The challenges are so formidable and the potential solutions so difficult to navigate. I hope for my own sake, for my children's sake, and for yours, that I am wrong.

PART 1

THE EUROPEAN UNION IN CRISIS

CHAPTER 1

EUROPE UNDER SIEGE

My starting point is to examine today's European Union in a wider context. While in the post-Cold War 1990s and 2000s, the European Union exuded a confident power of attraction that meant it could export stability to its surrounding neighbourhood, it is now importing instability, being probed and destabilised by hostile state and terrorist actors, and has lost the backstop that used to be provided by the United States. It is challenged, astonishingly, not only from the east and south, but also from the west.

THE CHALLENGE FROM THE WEST

Donald Trump is bad news for the European Union.[1] One can even go so far as to say he is a threat. He has engaged in the biggest populist questioning of the level of US commitment to Europe since World War Two. He has described NATO, which has much the same European membership as the EU and effectively acts as its hard security arm, as obsolete and largely irrelevant to today's main security threats, a view that has come as a surprise and a shock to many in Europe who are rightly worried about a reassertive Russia. He has frequently expressed his admiration for Vladimir Putin and has hinted at the wish to pursue a more cooperative relationship with him. He has been not only dismissive of the EU, but openly hostile to it. Trump welcomed the Brexit vote and declared that he'd like to see others follow the UK's lead and leave the EU. It seems obvious that he has not thought through what would follow in Europe were the EU actually to collapse. He welcomed Nigel Farage, the former leader of the UK Independence Party (UKIP), to Trump Tower just days after his election victory. He has called the EU a vehicle for German interests. His former chief strategist in the White House, Steve Bannon, has talked admiringly of the nationalist Le Pen family of politicians in France. His trade adviser, Peter Navarro, has suggested the US and Germany should be engaged in bilateral trade talks, essentially attempting to bypass the EU in one of its main areas of competence. And Trump has retweeted the racist venom of Britain First, showing either no understanding of, or no allegiance to, what used to be described as the shared values of the transatlantic space. His views are not only un-American, they are un-European.

Trump's various positions, moreover, are linked. If carried through into genuine diplomatic initiatives they would suggest a desire to remake the Euro-Atlantic economic and security order. For many east Europeans, to talk of a rapprochement with Putin while questioning NATO's *raison d'être* so soon after Moscow's annexation of Crimea is to table the prospect of a new Russian sphere of influence in eastern Europe. It is to suggest the future should be a carve-up resonant of Europe's past, not the EU's dream of an escape from it. It is to be the harbinger of a Europe where the great powers do as they wish while the smaller and weaker powers on the continent do as they must. Trump is an assault on the kind of Europe the EU was created to build.

The challenge Trump represents does not stop there. His positions with regard to the Middle East are also a threat not just to that region but to Europe. He has made clear that his primary goal is defeating ISIS militarily, but he is neglecting the parallel development of a political and diplomatic strategy to stabilise Syria and Iraq. He has mused about rejecting the two-state solution to the Israel–Palestine conflict, and has very controversially recognised Jerusalem as the capital of Israel. While the EU sits cheek by jowl with poverty and conflict on a massive scale to its south, Trump has cut the US aid budget and treats refugees as enemies. To the extent that his approach to the region is clear, it will increase the level of conflict in the Middle East, not reduce it, and it will be the EU that suffers the blow-back. Increased conflict will mean greater displacement of people, the triggering of a greater wave of migration and refugee flows, and an upsurge in terrorist activity. Eurosceptic populist parties salivate at the prospect. In that chaos they see an opportunity to rejuvenate their assault on the EU project as a whole and on the values it is supposed to embody. The result could be fatal to Europe's unity.

Trade is another area where Trump could do untold damage. The scrapping of the multilateral Trans-Pacific Partnership (TPP) negotiated by the Obama administration was one of his first acts as president. A threat to scrap the North American Free Trade Agreement (NAFTA) if it is not renegotiated to US liking remains on the table. And measures to force US companies to move investments in Mexico back across the border have been highly visible. Trump flirts openly with protectionism. If his relationship with it is consummated it will spell trouble for Europe's fragile economic recovery. Not only could it damage growth, exports and the bilateral trade relationship with the US but it could be toxic to the entire transatlantic political relationship. And if the Trump administration gets into a trade war with China, the EU will be put in an excruciating position. European–Chinese trade is itself huge and a dispute between the US and China would be one between the EU's two most important external trade partners. The assumption that Europe would simply side with the US, which would undoubtedly have been true for all of the last seven decades, can no longer be taken for granted, especially if the view in Europe was that the confrontation had been caused by ill-judged American belligerence rather than by the Chinese. Whichever way the EU and individual members of it chose to go, transatlantic relations would be badly damaged and with them, a host of European economic and security interests.

Trump already behaves as though continued military support to Europe must be 'paid for', and in the process implies that the security dimension of the transatlantic relationship is something akin to a protection racket. What store could be placed on US commitment to the defence of Europe if the EU and US were locked in a trade war and the EU was seen as being disloyal in a US trade confrontation with China? Without firm US support, a destabilised Europe that has underinvested in its own defence capability for decades will lie dangerously vulnerable and unable to act even when circumstances demand it.

The truth is that Trump represents a threat to the European Union at almost every level. His entire attitude to the EU and to trade is emblematic of a wider dismissal of multilateralism and multilateral institutions. He is hostile to collective efforts to tackle climate change. He is actively trying to undo the multilateral deal that has gained a measure of international control over the Iranian nuclear programme and that the EU was pivotal in helping to construct. He is dismissive of the United Nations. He represents a rejection of attempts to build and sustain a liberal, rules-based, international order, speaking admiringly of autocratic leaders who prefer to ignore it. He communicates no interest in protecting and preserving human rights, even going so far as to say that he supports torture himself. He peddles religious intolerance and when it comes to US behaviour on the world stage, including the use of American military power, he is utterly dismissive of the concept of international law. Trump's world is a world of raw power politics unconstrained by rules, and of transactional bilateral deals wherever they can deliver narrow advantage. There is no concept of wider American leadership responsibility, no sense of global leadership in defence of a more enlightened sense of self-interest. From the economic sphere to efforts to avoid major power conflicts, Trump rejects the ideas and institutions developed at the mid-point of the twentieth century as an answer to protectionism and devastating war.

Some have sought solace in his unpredictability, the argument being that it is more important to focus on what his administration does than on what he says. One can understand why. His unpredictability is a matter of public record. He has talked both about expanding the American nuclear arsenal and of seeking to reduce it; of binning the one-China policy but also of being committed to it; of no commitment to the two-state solution in the Middle East while indicating that he might be willing to support it.

Well over a year into his administration, large numbers of senior staff positions across the government were still to be filled, raising questions about Trump's ability to get much of anything done in practice, and when he has made senior appointments, the individuals involved appear to have views that are different to his own. Secretary of Defense Mattis, for example, takes a more hawkish view on relations with Russia than does Trump himself. But while for the optimist this all holds out the tantalising prospect that Trump will not be as damaging to European interests as at first appears, the reality is unlikely to be reassuring. First, the evidence suggests that when there is something Trump is clear about, like his desire to introduce the ban on refugees from certain countries in the Middle East, he is willing to expend considerable time and energy on doing what it takes to get it done. Second, the uncertainty on substance and lack of ability to get a well-staffed administration both point to the more alarming conclusion that either he doesn't know what he's doing or the insurgency he represents is so short of support in the policymaking establishment, including in the Republican foreign and defence policy establishment, that governing effectively at all is going to be beyond him. Far from limiting the damage Trump can do, this points to a likely diplomatic vacuum in any number of geographies and issue areas where American leadership has historically been important. Unless other democracies with progressive ideas, including in Europe, can step in to fill this gap, we are likely to see the interests and designs of several non-Western autocracies emerge as the winners.

At a point in its history, therefore, when the EU is vulnerable, the American people have served up not a friend to the European project, but a foe. A multiplier of instability in the European neighbourhood, a questioner of transatlantic security solidarity, a fillip to those who oppose it, and a source of turbulence in the international economy at a time when Europe needs to boost both growth and trade after nearly a decade of economic crisis. The EU also works best in a rules-based, soft-power, multilateral diplomacy system but Trump is a hard-power, aggressive-diplomacy president whose effect will be to contribute to a hard-power, aggressive-diplomacy world. The EU will find it harder to prosper both at home and abroad for as long as he is sat in the Oval Office.

THE CHALLENGE FROM THE EAST

Another leader who favours a hard-power, aggressive-diplomacy world is Vladimir Putin. He too is hostile to the European Union and a pretty good case can be made that he is trying to destabilise and destroy it with a mix of military and non-military means. Emblematic of this is a series of major 'snap' military exercises close to EU and NATO borders. One such, involving 80,000 ground, air and naval force personnel, practised war-fighting scenarios in the

Baltic Sea and in the Arctic close to the border with Norway. All militaries use exercises to prepare their readiness for real contingencies that may arise of course, but these exercises are designed to intimidate. They showcase the fact that Russia's revamped military is capable of rapid large-scale deployment, and what makes them so effective is the backdrop of real Russian military action in Ukraine. Russia annexed Crimea in March 2014 when it became clear that Ukraine favoured an association agreement with the EU over an agreement to join the Russian-led Eurasian Economic Union. It has since partially occupied and destabilised parts of eastern Ukraine using a mixture of support from irregular paramilitary forces there, and regular Russian forces when deemed necessary. Its message to the EU's eastern flank is: we can do the same to you.

The Russian military has also been engaged in a game of dangerous brinkmanship. It has used aggressive aerial manoeuvres, which have resulted in Russian and Western fighter aircraft coming within a few metres of each other in the air; mock cruise missile attack runs against targets in Denmark; submarine incursions off the coasts of Sweden and Scotland; and the abduction at gunpoint by Russian agents of an Estonian security service officer on Estonian, and therefore EU, territory. Its aircraft have also menaced civilian traffic. On 3 March 2014, a Russian warplane and a Danish civilian airliner came within seconds of a mid-air

collision just south of Malmö. The Russian plane was deliberately being flown with its transponders switched off and a
collision was avoided only because of evasive action taken
by the pilot of the civilian plane. Flight SAS 737, which was
carrying 132 passengers from Copenhagen to Rome, had a
lucky escape. Nine months later, on 12 December 2014, a
similar incident took place, again involving a Russian warplane with its transponders switched off.

Russian military operations have been accompanied by
the widespread use of fake news and cyber-operations across
a wide European geography. In November 2017, the UK
National Cyber Security Centre accused Russia of mounting cyber-attacks against Britain's energy networks and
telecommunications and media sectors. Researchers at the
University of Edinburgh concluded that 400 fake Twitter
accounts run from Russia had published posts about Brexit
in an attempt to influence the referendum on UK membership of the EU.[2] Attacks have been reported on the Danish
defence ministry and on the German parliament, the Bundestag. Just days before the German elections in September
2017, hundreds of Twitter accounts with links to Russia were
used to boost messages linked to the far-right party Alternative für Deutschland. And in the weeks running up to the
disputed referendum on Catalan independence in October
2017, Russian state-backed media organisations and auto-
mated social network accounts aggressively promoted fake

news stories about the actions of the Spanish authorities in an attempt to damage both them and public confidence in the democratic processes being used to make public decisions.[3] Polish government websites have frequently been attacked. Facebook pages supposedly dedicated to the creation of 'people's republics' in Polish-populated parts of Lithuania have appeared. Photos and political messages appearing on these pages exactly fit the template used by the Russians in Donetsk and Luhansk in Ukraine. Poland has also seen widespread use of Russian internet trolls, seeking to shape discussions in online forums. And in Finland, the web news editor of the newspaper *Helsingin Sanomat* has publicly talked about the large proportion of identical pro-Russian comments that are posted on its pages whenever a big news story about Russia or Ukraine breaks. These comments are consistently critical of NATO, the EU and the US.

But where Russian strategy excels is in its use of money. In what some have called the 'Kremlin Playbook', it funds the political activities of parties and groups inside the EU that are hostile to the EU's continuing existence.[4] It uses shell companies, offshore accounts and opaque company ownership regimes as channels through which to pass funds into the hands of EU political figures and to gain control of strategically important energy projects. And it uses initial low-cost injections of capital to secure multi-billion-dollar mega-deals in the EU energy sector only to subsequently use those deals to hike prices, and cream off wealth that can then be used to buy or reward the cooperation of those EU nationals willing to do Moscow's bidding. It uses, in other words, the corruption of individuals as a form of statecraft.

Occasionally, some of this activity finds its way to the surface. The most clear-cut case of Russian funding for a Eurosceptic populist party concerns the Front National (FN) in France. In 2014, Marine Le Pen's party reportedly received a €9 million loan from the First Czech Russian Bank, a financial institution with links to the Kremlin. The FN has aligned itself closely with a number of Russian positions, not least recognising the Russian annexation of Crimea and legitimising the subsequent referendum on Crimean separation by sending observers to monitor the vote. Leaked SMS messages indicated Le Pen's position on this, emerging through consultation with Russian officials.[5] In the same year, movements that peddle anti-Semitism and a neo-Nazi outlook, such as Jobbik in Hungary and Golden Dawn in Greece, were invited to a conference in Moscow hosted by an organisation close to Putin. The purpose of the conference was to discuss how Russian and other European 'national projects' could be better coordinated. Such moves have caused anger in Europe. Lubomír Zaorálek, the foreign minister of the Czech Republic, for example, openly accused Moscow of 'trying to divide and conquer the EU by funding movements across the continent'.

The case of Croatia-based Migrit Solarna Energija may also be instructive with regard to the Russian modus operandi.[6] In the summer of 2015, the company purchased a 14 per cent stake in Voimaosakeyhtio SF, a Finnish energy company involved in a consortium working to build a nuclear power plant in north-west Finland. The purchase was to facilitate a €158 million investment in the new nuclear plant by Migrit, without which the entire project might fall by the wayside because it was failing to meet the benchmark set by the Finnish government that at least 60 per cent of the capital behind it must be raised from within the EU. One of the biggest non-EU investors was Rosatom, Russia's state-owned nuclear corporation, which was set to build the new power plant's nuclear reactor. Given the high-profile nature of the project, and Finnish government rules, Migrit's involvement was the subject of some scrutiny. The project was suspended while investigations could be carried out into who owned and controlled the company. In July 2016, the authorities in Helsinki concluded that the ownership of Migrit Solarna Energija could not be 'adequately verified'. The economics ministry said it could not establish for sure that the company was 'factually controlled' from inside the EU. Herkko Plit, a senior civil servant, was quoted by the *Financial Times* as saying: 'We cannot speculate on who Migrit is controlled by. It has many relations to foreign countries, not just Russia. But … those people who founded it originally were Russians. The current owners are also Russian citizens to the best of our knowledge.' Olli Rehn, a former European commissioner who in April 2016 had become economics minister in Finland's right-wing coalition government, also confirmed to the Finnish broadcaster YLE that 'behind the Croatian company are Russian financiers'.

Just as the Finnish government was reporting its findings, Tomislav Karamarko, the former head of Croatian intelligence and high-flying first deputy Prime Minister of Croatia, was being forced to resign. He'd been caught up in, among other things, accusations of improper conduct involving payments made to a Germany-based economic think-tank from a foundation linked to the Croatian Democratic Union (HDZ), the political party of which he was a leading member. The problem was not the payments, which were all legal and only to pay for help in developing the HDZ's economic programme for the forthcoming elections, but where the money had come from. It is alleged Karamarko had, unbeknown to other senior members of the HDZ, accepted large amounts of money from an organisation called the Foundation of New Generations. That foundation in turn was linked in the Croatian press to none other than Migrit Solarna Energija.[7] In the space of just twelve months, it appeared Migrit may have been active in attempts to circumvent Finnish government investment rules, the purpose of which was to ensure EU interests controlled a strategically important energy project, and in trying to build a relationship with a senior Croatian government minister while, through a roundabout route, helping to meet the election expenses of his political party.

Questions also surround the PAKS-2 nuclear reactors project in Hungary. Although the four planned reactors have an estimated cost of €12.5 billion, something in the region of 10 per cent of Hungarian GDP, the contract to build them was awarded to Rosatom without bids being taken from other suppliers. Around €10 billion of the financing comes from Russia, via Vneshekonombank, which is close to the Kremlin, and at the time of writing remains under EU sanctions. Not only was the contract awarded in secrecy, but it is being shielded from public scrutiny. The Hungarian parliament has passed a law making everything about the deal confidential for as long as thirty years.

Russian strategy towards the EU is multidimensional. Its purpose appears to be to intimidate or otherwise secure the capture of individuals, institutions, projects and governments so they can then be relied upon to act in defence of Russian interests or be used to secure leverage that might in turn produce the same result. It appears to be driven by two sets of observations. The first concerns President Putin's basic analysis of how Russia has been treated by the West since the end of the Cold War. In a now infamous speech to the Munich Security Conference in 2007 Putin railed against the West for dismissing Russian interests and for behaving as though it was the sole arbiter of when an international intervention in a conflict somewhere was justified.[8] Putin sees the West as disrespectful to Russian sovereignty and he appears to believe the US and European governments are bent on trying to engineer his removal from office. His response has been to be far more assertive, especially in the Russian periphery. In 2008, relations between Russia and the West were set on a confrontational course when they were pitted against each other via the Russian–Georgian war, a development from which they have never recovered.

Second, however, Russian strategy seems to be informed by a very acute understanding of the European Union's own weaknesses. Putin knows that the 2008 financial crisis and subsequent sovereign debt crisis in the euro area caused economic chaos across the EU. He knows that that crisis contributed to the biggest questioning of the viability, credibility and legitimacy of the liberal order and Western market economies since the 1930s. He knows it weakened the ability of European states to invest in their own defence. And he has understood that against that backdrop, a degree of complacency has set in about the extent to which post-communist democratic consolidation in eastern Europe can been taken for granted. Where the EU's self-confidence in its own system and way of doing things has been undermined, Putin has seen an opportunity. Illiberal forces have come to the fore and Russian policy has been designed to help, encourage and profit from them. If they can be encouraged and even financed to disrupt EU and NATO unity, then the EU and NATO can be weakened and perhaps even brought to the point of disintegration, empowering Russia in the process and possibly delivering to it the sphere of influence in eastern Europe it has long desired. It is not an exaggeration, then, to say that Russian policy is one of war by other means, with the goal being not to defeat the EU in battle but to weaken its internal coherence and effectiveness so as to achieve victory without battle, in the military sense, ever being fully engaged in.

THE CHALLENGE FROM THE SOUTH

To the south, the threat to the European Union's cohesion and existence comes not from a single adversary but from the effects of a historical process. The old order in the Middle East has been unravelling, held together only by force and in many places not being held together at all. Some of the influences at play could usher in a future of more tolerant, open societies that has been longed for by many. But the ongoing turbulence and chaos are generating threats to the EU in the here and now. Threats that less than a decade ago it would have been difficult to imagine. Threats that can be illustrated by the story of one Abdelhamid Abaaoud.

At 10.28 p.m. on Friday 13 November 2015, at the lower

end of Boulevard Voltaire, Abaaoud exited a Paris Metro station and commenced a two-hour walk through the 10th and 11th arrondissements of the city. Over an hour earlier, he had been part of a group of attackers who had killed thirty-nine people at the restaurants La Belle Equipe, Le Carillon and Le Petit Cambodge. He had spent some time after those attacks driving a black Seat around the area close to the restaurants before being caught on CCTV cameras jumping the turnstile inside the Croix de Chavaux Metro station at 10.14 p.m. Abaaoud arrived at Boulevard Voltaire just as a second group of terrorists was in the process of slaughtering ninety people at the nearby Bataclan, a music venue packed with young concert-goers at the time. He was clearly drawn to the site of that massacre. Geo-location data on his mobile phone later showed that at 12.28 a.m., just as anti-terror police were entering the venue, Abaaoud was standing right next to them, taking in at first hand the chaos and bloodshed that he and his accomplices had unleashed on so many innocent people. Only a few minutes later, President Hollande was personally on the scene to examine the carnage for himself.

Abaaoud was no bit part player in this tragedy. He was the mastermind of the attacks that claimed 130 lives and left over 350 injured in Paris that night, and his biography is today's worst nightmare for every European intelligence agency. He was born in 1987 to a Moroccan father who had moved to

Belgium in 1975. His father had built a small business as a clothier in Molenbeek, a heavily Muslim-populated district of Brussels, and had sent his son to an exclusive Catholic school, the Collège Saint-Pierre d'Uccle, in a well-to-do part of the city. Abaaoud, however, was thrown out of that school and soon became involved in criminal activity. He first came into contact with the authorities in 2006 after drinking too much, posing as a police officer and threatening people with violence. He was detained, but only for a matter of days. Thereafter, he was frequently involved in drunken fights and on one occasion tried to break into a car repair shop, apparently while stoned. By 2012, he had already served a longer period in prison, and when he emerged in September of that year, he was sporting a beard and criticising the West for its behaviour in the Middle East. He told his lawyer that he had become religious and in the year that followed investigators believe Abaaoud was heavily involved in the jihadist scene in Belgium. In early 2014, Abaaoud kidnapped his thirteen-year-old brother and moved to Syria where, in a video made in Aleppo, the city in which he had joined ISIS, he said: 'All my life I have seen the blood of Muslims flow. I pray that God breaks the backs of those who oppose him.' According to the *Wall Street Journal*, while in Syria Abaaoud became an emir of war, 'an unusually high rank for a fighter who hailed from Europe'.[9]

On 29 July 2015, just a few months before the Paris attacks, a court in Belgium considering a case against a jihadist group convicted Abaaoud of terrorism-related offences in his absence and sentenced him to twenty years in prison. The judges argued that he had 'acted as if he were the head of a terrorist group' and that 'some elements [of his behaviour] gave cause for suspicion that he, *from either near or afar*, was a member of a cell that was preparing to commit an attack or attacks in Belgium'. The use of the phrase 'from either near or afar' was telling in two respects: first, because it indicated the authorities were not sure whether Abaaoud was in Belgium or Syria; and second, because it was assumed that even if he was in Syria, he could still pull the strings of a jihadist group operating in Belgium. Their assumption seemed soundly based. Court papers appeared to show strong jihadist links between the two countries. In one set of documents, the responsibilities of one of the Belgian defendants were described in great detail. These included: 'taking care of travel costs, accompaniment during the trip, contact to a smuggler who helps with the border crossing, reception at the border, training of fighters, assistance in leaving Syria, the transportation of personal objects and money belonging to jihadists, conveyance of news to the family, purchase and transportation of Belgian goods to Syria and the collection of donations'.

By October 2015, European authorities seemed clear that Abaaoud was in fact in Syria. The French expanded air attacks on ISIS targets there at around that time, apparently at least partly in an attempt to kill him. They thought they had met with success when reports began to circulate, and even reached his family, that Abaaoud had indeed been killed. That, however, was either just a mistake or a deliberately planted story to cover Abaaoud's tracks as he re-entered Europe.

Abdelhamid Abaaoud was eventually cornered by French police in the Parisian suburb of Saint-Denis five days after the attacks he had planned and launched on the Bataclan and other venues. After a gun battle that lasted several hours, he was killed with other accomplices in the apartment in which he was holed up. His body was reportedly bullet ridden and identification had to be carried out from his fingerprints.[10] Investigators soon discovered that Abaaoud had re-entered Europe via Greece, using a false identity and posing as one of the many refugees fleeing the war in Syria. He was not alone: several of his accomplices in the November 2015 Paris attacks had made the same journey. A Syrian passport found close to the body of a suicide bomber at the Stade de France, though containing a false photo, was later revealed to have been registered by authorities at every stage of its journey across Europe, starting in Greece, and passing through the Balkans and central Europe along what was by then a well-established route of entry for migrants and refugees to the continent.

The story of Abdelhamid Abaaoud and of the tragic events he was able to unleash therefore links two significant challenges to the cohesion of the European Union that are emanating from its south. The first is the threat of Islamist terrorism. The second is the major refugee and migrant crisis that has been impacting Europe since the spring of 2015. As Abaaoud's case makes clear, the Islamist terror problem is more home grown than imported but it is inextricably linked to events in the Middle East, where a list of grievances against the West, from the Israel–Palestine conflict to the military interventions in Iraq and Syria, are used to spread the message of holy war and to mobilise people to engage in acts of violence. This terrorist threat appears set to get worse now that ISIS has largely been defeated on the battlefields of Iraq and Syria and the thousands of other Abaaouds who travelled from Europe to become 'foreign fighters' for ISIS try to bring what they have learned back to the streets of Europe.

The migration and refugee crisis is every bit as challenging. The EU has in recent years faced the largest flows of migrants and refugees to Europe since the Second World War, not just from a Middle East in flames but also from a growing number of failed and failing states in Africa and central Asia. Although the quantities of both refugees and economic migrants arriving in Europe in recent months have not matched the dramatic flow that Abaaoud was able to hide within in late 2015, the challenge nonetheless remains a significant one today and for any number of reasons the numbers could yet begin to rise again.

Both separately and in combination, the terrorist threat and the migration and refugee challenge emanating from Europe's south have been seized on by populist and Euro-sceptic parties inside the EU, which have used them to stoke fear and fan the flames of intolerance. This is changing the character of public discourse, fuelling 'culture wars' and leading to an increased incidence of hate crime. The populists have been able to stimulate and tap into a well-spring of supportive attitudes across sub-sections of the EU population in doing so.

A 2016 Pew Research Centre survey of opinion in ten European countries laid some of this bare.[11] Across the countries surveyed, a median of 49 per cent said refugees arriving from places like Iraq and Syria posed a major threat to their own country's security. When the question was narrowed down to ask about terrorism in particular, the number went up to 59 per cent. Those on the right of the political spectrum were far more likely to hold these views than those on the left. In France, 61 per cent of those on the right said refugees were a threat, but only 29 per cent of those on the left agreed, a gap of 32 percentage points. The divide was reported at 30 percentage points in the UK, 29 in the Netherlands and 28 in both Germany and Italy. The apparent fear of refugees is strongly linked also to negative attitudes towards Muslims, who of course make up a large part of the current refugee and migrant flows into Europe. Commenting on the Pew Research, the analyst Bruce Stokes noted:

An unfavourable view of Muslims is held by majorities of people on the right in Greece, Italy, Hungary, Poland and Spain. And at least four in ten people on the right in Germany, the Netherlands and Sweden share that opinion … Again, there is a significant partisan divide in anti-Muslim sentiment: a 31-percentage point differential between those on the right and left in Greece, a 30-point difference in Germany, and a 29-point gap in Italy.

Studies by the UN have shown that migration does not make terrorism more likely. Many recent attacks in London and elsewhere have also been unconnected to migrants or refugees in any way. In the larger scheme of things, the numbers of migrants and refugees entering Europe ought to be manageable if EU governments cooperated to welcome and integrate them. A case could even be made that their arrival represents an opportunity to replenish a workforce that is otherwise going to suffer depletion through the effects of demographic change. But this has not been the predominant response. After an initial welcome from Chancellor Merkel in Germany and the heroic efforts of some smaller countries like Sweden, on balance, more countries in the EU have pandered to those who believe it is best to keep the migrants and refugees out. In doing so, they have contributed to a climate that has the potential to destroy the EU. If conditions in the Middle East and north Africa worsen and the numbers arriving go back up sharply, or if the terrorists succeed in mounting an attack of hitherto unprecedented proportions, it is likely that some ideas that are foundational to the European Union will be attacked and abandoned. A massive boost to political forces that want to see the EU dead would be no surprise. Laws that target whole social groups, such as Muslims, rather than respect the rights of every individual may well become commonplace. Border checks and fences may replace the Schengen free movement zone, amid claims by some interior ministry officials and law enforcement officers that in security terms Schengen leaks like a sieve anyway. If the EU cannot find answers that command citizen loyalty, remain true to its core ideals, and are also effective at addressing radicalisation and terrorism, it will remain dangerously close to the abyss. While Trump and Putin might weaken the EU and make it unsteady on its feet, the challenge from the south could deliver the knockout blow.

CHAPTER 2

THE ECONOMIC STORM

The story of Europe's economic and social crisis is first and foremost a story about people. It is the story of the Irish builder who, on the afternoon of 10 September 2010, blocked the gates of the Irish parliament with a cement mixer daubed with the words 'Toxic Bank'. His was a protest at the government's decision to leave *him* laden with debt while bailing out the country's banks. It is the story of early morning queues of young architects, business studies graduates and linguists outside employment offices in Spain, a lost generation condemned to idleness on a scale not seen in Europe since the Great Depression. And it is the story of countless Greek pensioners supporting entire families on €300 a month, supplemented by food grown in their own gardens, while thousands not even that lucky relied on volunteer food banks for survival.[12] It is the story too of an entirely different class of people. Of the politicians who were happy to milk the financial sector for tax revenues while understanding little of how the money was made. Of decision makers and officials who deregulated the banking sector without realising the risks they were running. And of the bankers who used deregulation to engage in an orgy of irresponsible lending, while often having no idea of the real risk positions being taken up by the banks they were supposed to steward. In all these personal stories lie the greed, irresponsibility, human suffering and tragedy of the European economic crisis of the last decade. In here too, in aggregate, is the story of how a crisis between bank creditors and debtors was ultimately turned into a catastrophically damaging confrontation between European nations and states.

THE PROMISE OF THE EURO'S FIRST DECADE

It was not intended to be this way. Monetary union, given that it represented one of the biggest voluntary transfers of sovereignty from states to a supranational entity in history, was supposed to be the ultimate symbol of Europe's solidarity. The final stage in the overcoming of the bitter divisions that had so scarred the continent's past. It was to help the poorer states in the EU catch up with the richer, and by removing the option of competitive currency devaluations as a means to address economic problems, to give a spur to reform of Europe's economies and make all of them more productive.

For a time, it worked. Bruegel, the Brussels-based economic think-tank, took stock of the euro's first decade in 2008, shortly before the global financial crisis and subsequent European sovereign debt crisis broke.[13] It concluded that while not everything in the eurozone garden was rosy, on balance the switch to a single currency had been a success. The introduction of the new currency on 1 January 1999 had been carried out smoothly. Further enlargements to include Greece, Slovenia and Cyprus had gone without a problem. For much of its first decade the euro area had enjoyed stable prices. Growth, while not spectacular, seemed to be picking up. And European financial markets were slowly becoming more integrated, a development thought to add resilience to any individual state that might suffer an economic shock. In global terms, a quarter of all foreign exchange reserves were held in euros. And Eurobarometer surveys showed that citizens inside the eurozone thought the single currency had made travel and a wide range of price comparisons easier and had made the European Union stronger in the world economy.

THE GATHERING STORM

As we now know, out of sight of this benign assessment, a storm that would shake the euro to its foundations was gathering. In 2006 and 2007, the bottom began to fall out of the US housing market. Borrowers who should never have qualified for a mortgage in the first place had started to default and banks heavily exposed in the mortgage-backed securities market began to lose money. America's fourth largest investment bank, Lehman Brothers, collapsed in September 2008, sending a wave of panic through global financial markets. Banks began to question not just the solvency of their non-banking clients but the solvency of each other. They stopped lending, driving those most heavily reliant on interbank lending for liquidity to the brink of collapse. In what quickly became a global crisis, European financial institutions were hit hard. The attempt to save them saw governments across the EU step in with offers of taxpayer-funded bail-outs. Between 2008 and 2011, €1.6 trillion, the equivalent of 13 per cent of the EU's annual GDP, was committed to this endeavour. But by intervening on this scale, European governments caused investors to turn their spotlights on to the strengths, or in some cases weaknesses, of those governments' deficit and debt levels. As Europe tipped into recession in 2009, negatively impacting public finances across the continent further, the pressure on European governments grew. Several found it exorbitantly expensive to take on new debt or to refinance existing debt and eventually some found it effectively impossible to borrow on the open market at all. What had started as a banking crisis had over time become a sovereign debt crisis and, as that crisis unfolded, it became an existential crisis for the euro itself.

The causes of this debacle were many. In hindsight, it seems obvious that the regulation of the US financial system, but also of the European and wider global financial system, was woefully inadequate. Politicians in charge at the time like to describe what happened as a banking crisis pure and simple. They are duplicitous in doing so. It was a banking crisis that took place in a regulatory context for which the political class, collectively, was responsible. Many banking executives and board members also behaved appallingly, either turning a blind eye to what they knew were deeply flawed lending practices or, worse, not understanding what they were in the first place. And then there are the national twists and particularities that give the story is texture. Greece was a country where profligate state borrowing and irresponsible state spending over a prolonged period resulted in disaster. It had joined the European Economic Community (EEC) in 1981 to pursue the dream of a more modern, prosperous economy and a more accountable form of government. It had done so only seven years after overcoming a long period of military dictatorship and had led the way for others, like Spain and Portugal, which were emerging from dictatorships of their own. Once in the EEC, however, Greece did not modernise. Its elites instead pursued a form of patronage politics with the left pumping benefits into special interest groups in the public sector while the right did the same for professional groups and for the military. Spending was systematically hidden from Greek taxpayers and from Greece's European partners by a form of organised deception for which the leaderships of the two main political parties were culpable.[14]

What works as an explanation for Greece's woes, however, does not work for other eurozone countries that subsequently found themselves in trouble and in need of help. Two of those countries, Ireland and Spain, actually had smaller deficits and debt at the start of the crisis than did Germany. For these countries, an entirely different dynamic occurred. A credit-fuelled boom in private, not public spending and borrowing, laid the path to ruin. The boom was facilitated by a global climate in which, from the late 1990s onwards, many banks and financial institutions massively increased their lending, but it also had a specifically European dimension, a dimension with its roots in German economic reforms carried out under Chancellor Gerhard Schroeder in the early 2000s. On entry into the euro Germany had been suffering high unemployment and was struggling to manage the effects of its reunification process. Schroeder introduced a series of controversial labour market reforms that reduced workers' rights, decentralised wage bargaining and weakened the power of the unions. One result was improved growth, largely on the back of rising exports to other parts of the eurozone. But another was that while capital flowed back into Germany, it did not flow into the hands of German workers. The reforms had resulted in an explosion of lower-paid, more precarious work and a long period in which real wages stagnated. With domestic demand suppressed and access to credit more tightly controlled than elsewhere in Europe, the German banks sought to put their capital to use by recycling it further into eurozone periphery countries such as Ireland, Spain, Portugal and Greece, where people took advantage of cheap credit to buy German exports and live beyond their means.[15] This recycling of capital from surplus to deficit countries is not, in itself, a problem. It was one of the benefits the euro was supposed to bring. The problem was not the credit flows themselves but the uses to which they were put, namely the stoking of unsustainable property bubbles in places like Spain and Ireland.[16]

POLICY FAILURE

This overall picture speaks to one of the other, and perhaps most important, underlying causes of the euro crisis, namely the weaknesses in the institutional, regulatory and political architecture of the euro that were present right from the start. The founders of the single currency knew about these and tried to manage them. The Maastricht Treaty, which led to the creation of the euro, introduced a set of supposedly mandatory commitments with regard to responsible management of the public finances. A state's entry and behaviour once in the single currency were supposed to be constrained by a stability and growth pact. This prohibited national deficits going above 3 per cent of GDP and limited the acceptable level of public debt to no more than 60 per cent of a state's annual income. The treaty also effectively banned eurozone member states from printing money to finance budget deficits and prohibited one member state from being held legally accountable for the debts of another, not only in future but also with regard to debts built up in the past. The idea that the single currency could be undermined by profligate spending in one, or more than one, member state, or that disciplined members might one day be forced to bail out the less disciplined had, it was thought, been handled.

Except it hadn't. What states signed up to and what they subsequently did in practice were far from one and the same thing. The stability and growth pact rules were never applied consistently. If they had been then Italy, Greece and Belgium would never have been admitted to the single currency in the first place. Even Germany just flagrantly ignored the strictures of the pact in 2004 by running a deficit larger than the rules allowed. And while the Maastricht Treaty gave member states protections against assuming each other's debt obligations in a legal sense, it gave no such protections politically. The single currency was, after all, supposed to be the ultimate symbol of solidarity among European states and when the crisis broke, the political pressure to help governments in trouble through voluntary interstate financial aid rather than through fulfilment of a treaty obligation was overwhelming.

This had major political consequences as the euro crisis unfolded. On the one hand it meant that the promise made to citizens in the EU's richer states, especially Germany, that membership of the euro would not lead to taxpayers bailing out governments in less well-off parts of the continent, was not kept. On the other, it meant that the reassurance given to citizens in poorer parts of the eurozone, that membership of the single currency would not result in a loss of control of economic decision making, was also exposed as flawed, because to get access to bail-out funds, their governments had to comply with conditions imposed on them from outside.

These problems with the eurozone's approach to managing fiscal policy were matched by others. More could have been done, for example, to address the problem of credit flows that were out of control. Interest rates are only one tool among many that governments can use to control flows of private credit, so the argument that governments of countries in the eurozone had their hands tied by a single interest rate does not hold water.[17] Steps could have been taken, for example, to increase the amount of money banks had to hold in deposit, relative to the amounts they were lending. Stricter rules could have been introduced to link mortgage offers to the size of income, and its proof, of those seeking to do the borrowing. Taxes could have been levied on banks that were lending too much. Even bankruptcy laws could have been used to make lenders think harder before lending, by making it clear that in settlement of such cases more of the lender's capital would be at risk.

The consequences of the failure to address such issues before the economic crisis were, if anything, dwarfed by the mistakes made once the crisis began. At a European Council meeting on 7 May 2010, eurozone leaders took a series of decisions that were to prove fateful not only for Greece but perhaps for the future of Europe as a whole. At that meeting the head of the European Central Bank (ECB), Jean-Claude Trichet, warned government leaders that if they did not stand behind eurozone states in trouble by pledging a sum similar to the $700 billion the US authorities had put into failing American banks, they might contribute to a market collapse similar in magnitude to that provoked by the demise of Lehman Brothers some twenty months earlier. There were serious reservations about Trichet's recommended course of action, especially in Germany, but he got his way. Eurozone leaders agreed to lend Greece €80 billion, with the support of another €30 billion from the International Monetary Fund (IMF). In addition, they agreed to facilitate €500 billion more to help other eurozone states coming under market pressure, a sum bolstered further by a promise of an additional €250 billion from the IMF, taking the total rescue fund available to €750 billion.

On the face of it these decisions demonstrated a level of intra-European solidarity in tune with the spirit of the entire

European integration project. Behind the scenes, however, was naked national self-interest and a decision to prioritise the interests of Greece's private sector debtors over those of the Greek and other taxpayers. Much of what Greece owed was to banks in Germany, France and other eurozone countries, and much of the money being lent was not to go to Greece at all but to be recycled directly to those banks to prevent them from suffering losses. The banking community's rhetorical commitment to the principle of moral hazard disappeared overnight, and a lot of taxpayers' money with it.

Despite that, to help manage political reservations about the bail-out, particularly in Berlin, it was stressed that the loan to Greece was conditional on Athens introducing major and very strict economic and social policy reforms. To ensure such reforms were implemented, a 'troika' of representatives from the ECB, the European Commission and the IMF conducted regular progress reviews before deciding on the release of each additional tranche of the loan to the Greek government. To say that the deal and the troika were both hated in Greece is an understatement. The point at issue was not whether reforms in Greece were needed, it was who was to call the shots in designing, leading and managing them. At a moment of profound national crisis with the country forced to face up to the need for radical change, the views of its population on what direction that change should take and how it should be implemented were effectively subordinated to those of unelected technocrats sent from Brussels, Frankfurt and Washington. The decision in 'lending' countries to privilege the interests of private creditors and their own banks over the interests of taxpayers while spinning that decision as a bail-out by one group of states of another also introduced and enshrined a political dynamic that pitted European states against each other.

Nor could it be argued that this whole approach was a necessary trade-off between democracy and a return to economic competence and prosperity, because the bail-out conditions actually had a counter-productive impact on the Greek economy. The theory was that the loan would keep Greece afloat while it cut back its expenditure to the point where it could once again command the confidence of lenders on the open market. Those same lenders, however, were not so much worried about Greece's budget deficit as its overall stock of debt, and since the assistance package agreed with Greece did nothing to reduce that debt, the Greeks were lumbered with massive debt service payments. Meeting them alongside the commitment in the bail-out agreement to run a primary budget surplus meant the government had to cut the deficit harder and faster than otherwise would have been the case. Cuts to pensions, public sector wages and other government expenditure reduced domestic demand and tax receipts. Subsequent strikes and protests damaged economic activity further. The whole package made it harder rather than easier for Greece to meet its debt obligations.

Despite this, the entire eurozone policymaking elite insisted there was no alternative and applied the same approach to other eurozone countries in trouble. Six months after the Greek bail-out, it was Ireland's turn to ask for help. As with Greece, the Irish government certainly bore much of the responsibility for the predicament in which it found itself. It had been incompetent in failing to rein in bank lending, complicit in allowing an unsustainable housing boom, and politically irresponsible in using the tax revenues from the boom to fuel it further. While it wasn't a government in debt when the crisis hit, with no deficit to speak of and total debt of only around 25 per cent of GDP in 2008, it couldn't therefore be described as a government in good standing either.

When the financial crisis struck and credit dried up, the bottom fell out of the Irish housing market and the debts of Ireland's banks quickly mounted. As bank failures loomed, the government compounded its difficulties by taking the same approach to the debts of its private banks as eurozone leaders had taken with regard to Greece. It operated on the basis that the repayment of money outstanding to its banks' creditors must take precedence over everything else. A blanket guarantee to honour all of its banks' commitments, worth almost three years of national income, was offered and billions of euros were poured into the banks to keep them afloat. The problem was that the more the Irish government did this the more the markets showed nervousness about Ireland's ability to actually make good on the guarantee. Those holding Irish government debt began looking to unload it and the rates that Ireland had to pay when issuing new debt rose sharply.

In the space of a few weeks in October and November 2010, two events crystallised not only the choice facing Ireland but the ideologically dogmatic response of the eurozone policymaking elite. First, in October, even as speculation mounted that Ireland would have to turn to the European Financial Stability Facility (EFSF) for help (the mechanism set up by eurozone leaders at their May 2010 crisis summit), the Irish government demonstrated both that it still had choices and that it was actively interested in trying to pursue them. What it did next offered what Martin Sandbu of the *Financial Times* has described as a tantalising glimpse into an alternative approach to managing the crisis. The Irish government forced junior bondholders of the failing Allied Irish Bank (AIB) to accept a reduction in the value of the bonds they held. In what can only be described as a ruthless move, it offered to reduce the value of bonds by 80 per cent for those bondholders who voted in favour of the move but by 99.999 per cent for those who voted against. Looming in the background was the threat of a full and forcible restructuring of the debt which could have left all the bondholders with nothing. The move worked and saved Irish taxpayers something in the region of €1.5 billion.[18]

No sooner had the government attempted to tentatively move down this alternative path, however, than it was bounced into reverse by the second event. On the morning of Thursday 18 November 2010, Patrick Honohan, the governor of the Irish Central Bank, called directly into the *Morning Ireland* radio programme from Frankfurt, where he was waiting to attend a meeting of the ECB. He announced that an outflow of funds from Irish banks by foreign institutions had created a need for financial support and that a rescue loan was being made available to Ireland, worth tens of billions of euros.[19] This was intended to pump capital into the banks and to put beyond any doubt the issue of whether the government had enough funds to meet its commitments.

This may or may not have been necessary to save the Irish banking system. The issue is a matter of dispute. In his book *Europe's Orphan*, Martin Sandbu argues that even at that point in the crisis Ireland had cash reserves for at least six months and a pension fund it could have raided to buy more time. It didn't need to go to the markets in the short term and could have used the time available to it to engage in further 'liability management exercises' of the kind just described at AIB, or to carry out an even more forceful write-down or restructuring of the debts of Irish banks. What is beyond doubt is that the democratically elected government of Ireland was bounced into a policy decision by the un-elected governor of its central bank. Out of sight of the public, the previous evening Honohan had tried to persuade Brian Lenihan, the finance minister, to bring cabinet colleagues together so they could agree to apply for a loan from the EFSF. Lenihan did not want to do this and was insistent that Ireland should avoid what he described as a Greek-style humiliation. Honohan's radio interview, however, publicly raised the spectre of an imminent banking collapse and the expectation of a rescue loan. Given that the warning came from an official of such standing, rejecting it would have caused market panic and a run on the banks. Within days Ireland had applied to the EFSF for a rescue loan and Ireland was subjected to the same troika treatment as Greece.

As in Greece, the rescue loan was recycled through to the irresponsible creditors of Ireland's banks, many of them other European banks. These were creditors who had fuelled the unsustainable boom years by lending to Ireland's banks with little regard for or assessment of risk but they had their interests prioritised over the Irish taxpayer regardless. As a result of this, and as a result of the government's need to recapitalise the banks as well as honour their debts, Ireland's debt, just 25 per cent of GDP at the start of the crisis, was 124 per cent of GDP by 2013.

Even this is not the end of the story. The most insidious aspect of both the Greek and Irish cases was not the rescue loans themselves and the conditions attached but the way in which they were enforced. While the role of the troika in each case was humiliating for both government and people alike, and in the case of Greece in particular it did flex its muscles to keep the pressure on for internal labour market and other reforms, in the end it was not the main enforcer. That role fell to the ECB. This is because when a bank is in trouble it needs a fresh influx not only of equity to compensate for its losses but also of liquidity capital to refinance short-term debts coming due on a regular basis. In both Greece and Ireland the government provided the former to struggling banks and it was the job of the ECB to provide the latter. It did so, but again, only on certain conditions.

Before dwelling on what those conditions were, it is important to spell out what the consequences are for an economy and society if the liquidity tap is switched off. Essentially, without access to that short-term finance from the central bank, a country's banks run out of cash. Families and businesses cannot access savings, pensions or capital. They cannot pay bills. A run on the banks accelerates the process of collapse. In that scenario, a government can either impose capital controls on banks, which is to say they ban people and businesses from taking money out of the bank, or they can provide an additional source of liquidity: they can print money.

As part of the rescue agreement between Ireland and

the rest of the eurozone, the ECB agreed to keep providing liquidity to Irish banks but only on condition that they engage in no further liability management exercises (bail-ins), restructuring or writing down of the debts owed to the banks' creditors. In other words, the ECB effectively threatened to try to force Ireland out of the euro, to force it to print its own currency to provide liquidity, if it didn't agree to do what the bank wanted. It used the same threat repeatedly in relation to Greece but this time to protect not primarily the creditors of the banks but the holders of Greek sovereign debt, and to ensure the reforms insisted on by the troika were introduced. In June 2015, at one of the high points of the crisis between the radical Syriza government in Athens and eurozone leaders, the ECB actually did switch off liquidity to Greece's banks, forcing the government to introduce temporary capital controls.

Defenders of the ECB's approach will point out that it has a responsibility not to continue lending to insolvent banks. That is true. But the ECB's condition for maintaining liquidity flows in each case was not that the banks to which it was lending be made solvent. It was that they be made solvent in a very particular way, by massive injections of taxpayer funds rather than through the write-down or restructuring of debts owed to creditors. It totally overstepped the mark in terms of the legitimate role of a central bank and insisted on telling elected European governments what to do with taxpayer funds while implicitly threatening to expel them from the single currency if they did not comply. In doing so, it was supported by pretty much the whole eurozone policymaking elite, which insisted there was no alternative. A similar approach to managing the crisis was imposed on Portugal. A few months after Ireland found itself in trouble, Lisbon was struggling to meet its refinancing costs on international bond markets. With the ECB once again threatening to cut off emergency liquidity support to Portuguese banks, the government was forced to accept the same programme of a taxpayer bail-out of banks, deep austerity, structural reforms and supervision by the troika.

Alongside the deeds of the ECB, in Germany Chancellor Merkel was working to turn the approach to fiscal policy applied to the crisis countries, namely cuts, into a eurozone-wide approach. First through bilateral diplomacy with President Sarkozy in France, and then through the European institutions, she insisted on far tougher spending rules for euro member states. These were encoded in the Treaty on Stability, Coordination and Governance in the Economic and Monetary Union, or what became known colloquially as the Fiscal Compact. I will return to the issue of the Fiscal Compact later in the book. For now, it is sufficient to note that it gave new powers to the European Commission to inspect and reject planned national budgets and to levy hefty fines on any transgressors.

In adopting this line, Chancellor Merkel was undoubtedly responding to a domestic political environment in Germany in which the bail-out agreements were very unpopular. She needed to show German taxpayers that they would not be on the hook for an endless stream of similar bail-outs in future. But understandable as that may be, it didn't mitigate the counter-productive consequences of the whole approach. The combination of severe bail-out terms for the countries facing the brunt of the crisis with eurozone-wide spending cuts to meet the terms of the Fiscal Compact drove the eurozone as a whole deeper into recession. A further decision not to cleanse the banking system of bad debts but to maintain the fiction that one day all of those debts would be repaid left Europe with a series of zombie banks. The operations of these banks made the credit crunch worse because they were reluctant to lend for fear they might one day need the capital they did have to make good on assumed but as yet unrealised losses.

The various strands of eurozone policy also fed off each other. As economies shrank, debt-to-GDP ratios increased, making it harder for states to service existing debts and raising questions about their ability to do so in the minds of investors. When precisely this dynamic began to affect two of Europe's largest economies, Spain and Italy, in the summer of 2011, not only did the effective interest rate these governments had to pay to borrow go through the roof but the value of bonds issued by them plummeted. Since many of those bonds were held by their own banks, the balance sheets of Spanish and Italian banks were damaged further, raising continued questions about the banks' own viability and reinforcing their already stifling reluctance to offer new credit to support productive economic activity. Into that dynamic, Jean-Claude Trichet sent further missives to Prime Ministers Zapatero of Spain and Berlusconi of Italy on 5 August 2011, demanding that the whole policy package applied elsewhere in the eurozone be fully implemented in these two countries. This time, the threat from the ECB was not to turn off liquidity to the banks if they did not get compliance but to refuse to buy Italian and Spanish government bonds to keep them afloat.[20]

It is no exaggeration to say that the decisions of eurozone policymakers, and their associated mantra that there was no alternative, had taken the most severe economic and financial crisis for decades and made it worse. And it is this fallacy, the fallacy that no alternative existed, that perhaps did more damage to the ideal of European integration than any other development in recent decades. The next chapter considers the social and political consequences. For now, it is important to spell out what the alternative was.

AN ALTERNATIVE APPROACH

Officially, the argument of eurozone officials was that a decision to inflict losses on senior creditors of a European bank would trigger a run on other banks in the eurozone as investors concluded nowhere was safe. Patrick Honohan went as far as to assert that taking this course of action would trigger a 'European Lehman' and in doing so, he spoke for most ECB colleagues and the European Commission. Leaving aside the dubious comparison of one of the Irish or Greek banks with that of Lehman Brothers, a bank central to the overnight lending market between banks and with a balance sheet measured in the trillions of dollars, this assertion of systemic risk is notable for two reasons.[21] First, while pointing to systemic risk, its proponents used that argument not to mount the case for a systemic international response but to determine that it was taxpayers in the bail-out countries alone who should pick up the full tab for saving the system as a whole. Second, it is dubious because not only are there ways of conducting the orderly restructuring or resolution of failing banks but some of those procedures have been used without causing the contagion of which Honohan spoke.

These so-called 'special resolution regimes' are effectively the means by which a failing bank can be carved up to separate out its remaining good assets from the bad. Some of the good assets are then used to back the continued operation of the bank's essential functions, namely maintaining credit flows to worthy clients, allowing deposit accounts to be used as a trusted place to store value, and managing the electronic payments system to allow transactions to take place. The remaining assets, once this has been done, are left to be shared by the bank's remaining creditors, some of whom may routinely be given equity in the new 'good' bank, in return for taking losses on some or all of the money they were owed.

At about the same time as the Irish government was giving its guarantee to stand behind all of its troubled banks, the Icelandic government was facing the total melt-down of its banking system. The three banks that dominated the domestic market were bankrupt and the Icelandic national bank had nothing like the hard currency reserves required to help them stay afloat. They were simultaneously too big to fail and too big to save. The government in Reykjavik did the only thing it could do in the circumstances. It separated the national from the foreign parts of the banks, moved the domestic elements of the balance sheet into new nationalised entities and allowed the foreign parts of the banks to go bust. Foreign creditors suffered losses and the economy as a whole took a big hit, but no bigger than that experienced in euro-zone countries taking the troika and ECB medicine, and the domestic banking system continued to function. Icelandic taxpayers were also left with far less debt. No contagion followed.[22] This was not the only case. The Danish authorities put the Amagerbanken bank through a similar procedure shortly before Honohan's momentous phone call to *Morning Ireland*.[23] The government took the bank over, wrote down debts to junior creditors entirely and made senior creditors take a 41 per cent reduction in what they were owed. The entire operation was carried out over a single weekend and by Monday morning a new bank was not only in existence but functioning normally. The Danish government had to pick up the bill for some guaranteed bonds and the national deposit insurance scheme made sure small depositors did not lose out, but the costs were manageable and beyond a small increase in borrowing costs for other Danish banks, there was no wider impact on the banking system.

There have been other examples historically too, of course, because banks do occasionally go bankrupt. And lest anyone think the claim that Europe's crisis could and should have been managed with a far greater emphasis on such an approach is a claim made only by those uninitiated in the ways of finance, two other points are worth noting. The first is that the International Monetary Fund supported the idea that resolutions on some of Europe's banks were necessary at the height of the crisis but was overruled by the European members of the troika. The second is that eurozone leaders, faced with the consequences of their own decisions, have increasingly had to acknowledge the case as the crisis has gone on. By 2012, the policy prescriptions being offered had not only failed to stabilise the situation but had fuelled further speculation that the euro might collapse. A second bail-out for Greece was agreed in March 2012 but this one came with a difference. As part of the package, a voluntary agreement was reached with some (though not all) of Athens's creditors to the effect that about €100 billion would be written off the face value of the bonds they held, and on the remainder, not only would interest rates be kept low, but the repayment period would be extended over decades. No contagion followed but some of the losers in the write-down were major banks in Cyprus.

This, along with the effects of a recession and associated housing slump, had left the two biggest banks in Cyprus effectively bankrupt. What followed exposed not just the political and moral bankruptcy of the eurozone approach to the crisis but the extent to which commitment to that approach could be tempered by the demands of political expediency. Cyprus introduced a new element into the mix because its banks were known to be a haven for Russian money. Nevertheless, eurozone leaders, worried about the costs of pursuing their previous approach to rescuing the banking system, signed up to a deal that, in return for modest bail-out funds, would impose a levy on *all depositors* in Cypriot banks, whether they be Russian billionaires or ordinary Cypriot citizens with small deposit accounts. This was the deal the Cypriot government itself wanted, because it wanted to preserve its status as an offshore financial centre. Not only, however, did it preposterously violate supposed EU legal protections for those with deposits of €100,000 or less, but it put European taxpayer funds on the table to help reduce, though not eliminate entirely, the hit on Russian dirty money.

When the deal collapsed because of the sheer outrage and protests it generated in Cyprus itself, the hypocrisy with which the ECB had previously claimed there was no alternative in Ireland and Greece was rammed home.[24] It now agreed to the deal being modified, to reinstate protections for all depositors with less than €100,000 in savings, and increased the hit to larger depositors.[25] It did provide some bail-out funds but threatened to turn off liquidity to Cypriot banks – not to make sure they agreed to make good on all their debts to their creditors, but to make sure they didn't. To keep the financial taps turned on, the reluctant Cypriot government *had* to agree to restructure the banks and inflict losses on creditors, exactly the opposite of what had been demanded of Greece, Ireland and others.

Ultimately, the measures introduced as part of Greece's second bail-out in 2012 and in the Cypriot bail-out in 2013 were steps in the right direction. They were added to by a gradual loosening of austerity from late 2012 on, and also by more positive steps taken by Mario Draghi, who had replaced Jean-Claude Trichet as head of the ECB in November 2011. Among other measures, Draghi lowered interest rates, offered the banks longer-term ECB loans and found a way to buy on the open market unlimited amounts of sovereign bonds of any country that had had a rescue loan from the European Stability Mechanism (formerly the European Financial Stability Facility). Collectively, these measures improved the economic picture in the eurozone overall. But they were reluctant steps and didn't go far enough, particularly with regard to bank debt restructuring. Pains were taken to show that the write-downs of debt in relation to Greece and Cyprus should not be seen as setting a precedent for other cases in future. They did not represent a full volte-face but a messy policy evolution. And as the next chapter makes clear, the social and political damage arising from eurozone policy had already been done.

CHAPTER 3

SOCIAL PAIN, POLITICAL CONSEQUENCE

One of the defining political features of the decade of European crisis has been the challenge to mainstream orthodoxies mounted by a series of political outsiders, some from the right, some from the left. This populist challenge has been years in the making but it really began to explode into wider public consciousness in 2014. That was the year in which the UK Independence Party (UKIP) won more votes than any other political party in Britain in the European elections. Early the following year, the radical left Syriza movement won the general election in Greece. And throughout 2015, political support for some radical right-wing movements also began to increase markedly. Marine Le Pen's Front National scored a stunning success in France's local elections, winning six of the thirteen regions being contested. Left-wing parties, in the form of Podemos in Spain and the Left Bloc in Portugal, came either from nowhere or from years of relative obscurity to have a major impact on national politics in their respective countries too. At the UK general election, the Scottish National Party won almost every seat in Scotland and decimated the Labour Party, which had previously been dominant there.

From a British perspective, even this was only a warm-up. In June 2016, the UK voted to leave the European Union in a referendum that was called at least partly because UKIP was seriously outflanking David Cameron's Conservative Party on the right. Cameron had made the promise of a referendum in 2013, having become convinced that in the context of UKIP's rise, it was the only way to both preserve Conservative Party unity and to shore up his own electoral position ahead of the 2015 general election. Elsewhere and more recently, in 2017, Europe's political elite breathed a sigh of relief when in the Netherlands the Party for Freedom, led by Geert Wilders, lost an opinion poll lead during the course of the election campaign and came only second in that country's national election. Emmanuel Macron's defeat of Le Pen in France was a further boost to confidence. Some also point to Ireland as a country where populism has failed to take hold. But none of these cases is completely convincing. France is dealt with at length later in the book. In Ireland, a plausible case can be mounted that no new populist party has emerged because populist policies have flowed into the mainstream.[26] And the

agenda set out by Wilders in the Netherlands totally dominated the election debate there. To win, the incumbent Prime
Minister, Mark Rutte, had to significantly shift his policy positions to the right, and the Party of Freedom's second place
was the party's best ever election result. The mainstream and
long-standing Dutch Labour Party was annihilated in what
became a contest not between traditional left and right but
between the right and the far right. In the 2016 presidential
election in Austria, the far-right candidate, Norbert Hofer,
came within 31,000 votes of winning. The populist Law and
Justice Party is the government in Poland. In Italy, throughout 2017 the populist Five Star Movement led the polls
consistently. Even in the Nordic region, that many Europeans like to see as a bastion of progressive social attitudes and
policies, the populists have had their effect. The Finns Party
in Finland managed to make itself the second largest party
and to play a role in government for a time by combining
left-wing economic policies with social authoritarianism and
ethnic nationalism. The Sweden Democrats, also far right,
have gone from nowhere to polling almost 20 per cent support in under a decade.

There is a lively debate about what has driven this new
populist phenomenon. Some argue that its roots have less
to do with European specifics and more to do with a wave
of globalisation and technological change that has led to
stagnant wages and precarious employment in parts of

the developed world. For those of this persuasion, nothing could be more illustrative of the fact that we are dealing with trends that go well beyond Europe than the election to the US presidency of Donald Trump. His campaign rhetoric on the need to protect American workers from unfair global competition could not have been more explicit. And even if one believes, as important thinkers like James Bessen do, that the next wave of technological innovation and automation may well create more jobs than it destroys, who today would deny that job insecurity and static or declining real-terms wages are an important part of the picture?[27] For others, this narrative must be balanced with one focused on the rise of identity politics. The debate can be heated, and not necessarily all that productive. It is clear that identity politics is important and that fear of societal change underpins much concern about levels of immigration, but I have yet to come across a form of identity politics that didn't try to mobilise support by claiming it was the answer to people's underlying social and economic concerns.

What seems clear is that both economic insecurity and identity politics have been influential in damaging and in some cases destroying what might be described as pre-crisis mainstream politics. What also seems clear is that events in Europe over the last decade have given the populist phenomenon there a boost. Every one of the facets of Europe's crisis touched upon in previous chapters has a claim to significance in explaining the rise of what Steve Richards has labelled 'the outsiders'.[28] Central themes of European populists of both left and right, for example, have been that the elites have left too many people behind and that Europe is not being run for 'the people'. To understand why that claim might resonate, it is important to think not only about the economic statistics born of the euro crisis, important though they are, but also of the human stories and social impacts they represent.

THE HUMAN AND SOCIAL COST OF THE EURO CRISIS

One story, captured by the aid organisation Caritas Europa, offers a window on the hardship suffered by many. Marek moved from Poland to Greece in 1991. He has since had three children, all born in Greece, and now performs the near-heroic task of raising them alone. He is a builder by trade. From 1991 to the start of the financial crisis he worked in construction. He and his children lived well. When the crisis came, however, he lost his job and has been unemployed for most of the time since. He spends his days looking for work, picking up perhaps four or five days of casual work each month. He describes how his first priority is the bills and the children's food, and after that, the rent. When he goes to the supermarket, he buys the bare necessities and the cheapest of everything.

Marek also has a heart condition. For more than a year he was unable to afford the €100 a month required to buy the medication he should have been taking, nor could he pay for all the tests the doctors recommended to further diagnose his condition. As someone who was long-term unemployed, he lost his health insurance cover. Over time, the church and charities like Caritas have helped him with food parcels and have paid both for his medication and for his medical tests. Friends have helped him by passing on old clothes for his children. But his situation is desperate and there is no prospect of improvement. The only thing that comforts him and keeps him going is his children. He believes he is fortunate in that they understand how serious the situation is. They have matured early and don't ask him for things they know he cannot buy. When they see him worried, they hug him and comfort him. That, he says, is what keeps him from giving up.[29]

There are literally millions of stories like Marek's across Europe, such has been the devastating and Europe-wide impact of the economic crisis and its mismanagement by eurozone elites. The initial effect of the stimulus to European economies introduced after the onset of the financial crisis in 2008 lifted the continent out of a deep recession. The eurozone economy grew at a rate of around 2 per cent over the two-year period from the first quarter of 2010 to the final quarter of 2011. Once the effects of the subsequent retrenchment and prescription of austerity as a solution to the sovereign debt crisis had kicked in, however, the euro-zone was tipped back into recession. This second and deeply damaging recession lasted for eighteen months from the beginning of 2012 to the middle of 2013. And even after that, growth crawled along for years at less than 1 per cent.

ECONOMIC AND SOCIAL CONSEQUENCES

The consequences of the policies introduced to manage the sovereign debt crisis had differential economic and social effects across Europe, but just about everywhere they were serious. Marek's story was a tiny part of the wider Greek tragedy. Greece went into recession in 2008 as the global financial crisis began. Its economy shrank by 0.2 per cent in that year. It then went on to shrink by 3.1 per cent in 2009, 4.9 per cent in 2010, 7.1 per cent in 2011, 6.4 per cent in 2012 and 3.2 per cent in 2013. Between 2008 and 2013 it experienced a six-year recession that the IMF has described as one of the deepest peacetime developed-economy recessions in history. It was, in fact, a deeper and longer slump than that endured by the United States in the Great Depression. Even in 2014, Greece barely crawled to only 0.3 per cent growth and in 2015 its economy shrank again.

The crisis led to the dismantlement of Greece's social safety net. The national minimum wage was reduced by 22 per cent for the over-25s and by 32 per cent for the under-25s.

Unemployment benefits were cut and means testing was introduced. Rent subsidies were suspended, VAT increased, and excise duty placed on fuel. Pensions and public-sector pay were slashed. Collective bargaining procedures were dismantled and labour laws were changed to make it easier for employers to fire workers. Notification periods for those being made redundant were also shortened and severance pay reduced.

By mid-2013, unemployment in Greece had risen to almost 30 per cent. The proportion unemployed for more than a year represented 60 per cent. Youth unemployment also was running at over 60 per cent and those not in education, employment or training accounted for 20 per cent. The rise in unemployment was particularly painful because unemployment benefits cease after twelve months in Greece and people out of work for that amount of time also lose entitlement to health insurance. One 2013 estimate showed that 800,000 people, like Marek, had lost health insurance cover as a result of the crisis. More fees and co-payments have been introduced to the health care system, and closures of hospitals and health centres have compounded the problem of worsening access to health care.

Not surprisingly, poverty has sky-rocketed. There has been a big increase in the number of households with no one in work. Many households report being unable to pay their rent or afford heating in winter. There has been a dramatic rise in homelessness, and a significant rise in both malnutrition and mental health problems. The suicide rate has gone up, and births have dropped by 10 per cent while still-births have increased by over 20 per cent. Children have suffered in particular. The number of primary school age children suffering from malnutrition has increased sharply, and services for children with disabilities or mental health problems have been drastically cut.

Amid its economic and social crisis, Greece has been on the receiving end of the flows of refugees and migrants escaping the conflict zones and poverty of the Middle East, Africa and central Asia. This has both increased the number of undocumented migrants and their children entering Greece and fed a growth in the phenomenon of people living in dangerous, often abandoned, buildings. The presence of large numbers of migrants in the midst of extant social and economic stress has fed an increase in xenophobic and racist attacks on foreigners. It is not surprising, given this overall context, that the Parliamentary Assembly of the Council of Europe has described the situation in Greece as a humanitarian crisis.

In Italy, where high levels of government debt before the crisis made the country particularly susceptible to concerns about debt serviceability, austerity produced a serious recession by the spring of 2011. Cuts were introduced to the health and social services provided by regional and local bodies and at the national level to health, education and social benefits programmes. The public sector was cut back in size and funding, the link between pensions and the cost of living was severed to keep costs down, and VAT was increased on a range of essential goods, disproportionately damaging the incomes of the poor. Pension cuts had a particularly damaging effect on a country where the incomes of the older generation play a significant role in overall extended family budgets and on cash transfers that take place to the young. Unemployment rose to over 12 per cent, or around three million people. More than half of these were long-term unemployed (unemployed for more than a year). The unemployment rate among the young rose to over 35 per cent. By 2012, those living in poverty or social exclusion in Italy were estimated to number a staggering 18.5 million people. In a country where the national stereotype is of fondness for children, the high commissioner for human rights of the Council of Europe warned that austerity had increased the risks of child labour and exploitation. A UNICEF ranking of child well-being showed Italy ranked twenty-second out of twenty-nine countries examined.

Spain, which unlike Italy entered the crisis with very low levels of government debt (at only 36 per cent of GDP in 2007), quickly found itself engaging in similar policies to those of Italy, and with similar effects. The bail-out of Spanish banks affected by collapsing property values saw a massive rise in Spain's year-on-year budget deficit and an increase in its debt-to-GDP ratio to around 100 per cent by 2013. The EU leaned on Spain to pursue austerity and the country returned to recession. Health and social care budgets were cut at a time when demand was increasing. VAT was increased. Changes to labour laws were introduced to help employers make workers redundant more easily. Unemployment rose to unprecedented levels in Spain's history. By 2013, it was over 25 per cent, or around six million people. Almost half of this unemployment was long-term. Youth unemployment topped 50 per cent, despite very high levels of emigration among the young. As a statement of the scale of a country's past failure and of the lack of promise afforded by its likely future, this was a devastating indictment.

Even in Ireland, which fared much better than some others, the situation has been dire. Ireland enjoyed almost no growth at all between 2007 and 2013. The measures it took to bail out its banks saw its debt rise from less than 30 per cent of its GDP in 2007 to 132 per cent in 2013. Between 2008 and 2014 there were no fewer than nine austerity budgets. These sought to rein in spending and debt through a combination of spending cuts and tax rises with the former taking the lion's share of the burden. Education, health, social care and benefits budgets were all hit hard as a result. Officially, unemployment increased to around 15 per cent in 2014 and has since fallen slightly. However, the country has also seen large-scale emigration as a result of the crisis, especially among the young. Along with large numbers of people who have become discouraged from entering the labour market and therefore don't show up in the figures, this led the IMF to estimate that the real unemployment rate was more like 24 per cent. Even among those getting work, the evidence shows that much of it is part time among people who want to work full time.

All across the eurozone the effects of the initial and catastrophic approach to the sovereign debt crisis were felt. The Netherlands, Austria, Finland, Sweden, Denmark, Hungary, Slovenia, the Czech Republic, Portugal, and Belgium all fell back into recession. Bulgaria flatlined. Croatia endured a six-year recession all the way through to 2014. France bounced along with almost no growth. In fact, between 2008 and 2016 France grew at an average rate of only 0.6 per cent. Even this figure is only as high as it is because of the two years of almost 2 per cent growth experienced in 2010/11 on the back of the original post-financial crisis stimulus introduced before the eurozone turned to austerity.

Alongside the double-dip recession inflicted on much of the eurozone, a number of other common themes emerged as a result of the twin-track policy framework of bail-out and austerity that was adopted as a solution to the crisis. The first was that the burdens of adjustment were disproportionately heaped on the poor and those least able to bear the cost. One OECD report suggested that in Ireland, the poorest 10 per cent of households had lost twice as much of their disposable income as the top 10 per cent. In every country where austerity has been pursued, cuts to public services have also disproportionately affected the poor who rely on those services the most.

The second theme was that the economic downturn negatively affected the banking system. In Greece, for example, the combination of falling wages, rising unemployment and tax increases all reduced incomes and increased the rate of non-performing loans held by the banks. Across the eurozone, the number of non-performing loans held by banks grew. This meant that a question mark continued to hang over the viability of some of those banks and also that banks hoarded whatever capital they did have while being reluctant to invest in new economic activity. A negative feedback loop between states' reluctance to invest in growth because of the fiscal circumstances brought on by the bail-out of the banks, and banks' reluctance to invest in economic activity because of their own fragility and lack of confidence in future demand, generated a persistent problem of low investment across the eurozone. This problem persists to this day. Alongside a loss of productive skills among the large numbers of long-term unemployed and the underdevelopment of skills among the huge numbers of young unemployed, it is one of the primary reasons why the eurozone has struggled to mount a robust recovery after crawling out of recession towards the end of 2013. The eurozone's post-crisis recovery has, in fact, been one of the slowest on record and is much slower than that enjoyed by the United States.

In 2017/18, France, Germany and Italy are all projected to enjoy growth, but of around or below 2 per cent and, in the case of Italy, barely above 1 per cent. Spain is doing better and both its own political leaders and many in Europe's wider political establishment would like to see it viewed as proof that the austerity and reform medicine is working. However, Spain only returned to pre-crisis levels of economic output in 2017. Nine years after the financial crisis started, it has returned to where it was in 2008. While unemployment has started to fall, standing at around 18.5 per cent in mid-2017, it remains far above its pre-crisis level and almost double the eurozone average. There is a new class of working poor in the country, and inequality has increased dramatically. Spanish government debt remains at 100 per cent of GDP. To the extent that Spain stands out (and one would need to be looking through strange glasses indeed to define it as an economic success, as some in the eurozone would have us do), most analysts believe that this is less to do with austerity and more to do with the fact that alongside its bail-outs of banking institutions, it has indeed restructured some of them, shutting down ones that couldn't survive, recapitalising others, and moving most of the bad assets into a bad bank. This has all meant balance sheets were cleaned up, loan loss provisions fell and markets regained trust in the banking system more quickly. Credit has been flowing far more effectively to Spanish businesses than to Italian ones as a result. It is this, more than anything else, that explains the difference in the more recent economic performances of the two.

The overall economic consequence of the pursuit of austerity and a failure to restructure failing banks thoroughly enough across the eurozone has been to make Europe poorer than it otherwise would have been. Socially, it has increased poverty and inequality to unnecessary and unfair levels and has inflicted massive pain on individual and family lives that have been wrecked in the process.

The link between this economic and social context in Europe and the increasing success of populist political movements seems undeniable. The only surprise perhaps is how long it took after 2008 for the public anger to find concrete political form. Even now, it is central bank leaders like Mark Carney, worried about the legitimacy of the entire economic system, who are taking the lead in pushing more mainstream political leaders and labour unions to go further in response.[30]

Populists of both left and right have been explicit in using the economic crisis and its effects to fuel their case. On the right, they have promised to address the crisis by acting to protect domestic industries and jobs from cheap and unfair overseas competition. They have promised big spending increases on infrastructure, on welfare and often on the military. Marine Le Pen is a good example of the genre. She promises to shield French workers from globalisation, to put taxes on imports to France, to boost defence spending and to lower the retirement age while increasing a wide range of welfare payments. Her welfare agenda finds a strong echo in the Danish People's Party. It is also explicit about being willing to defend the extensive welfare benefits that Danes enjoy, though it says this can only be afforded by limiting the number of immigrants entering the country and therefore able to gain access to the system. Right-wing populists in Europe also rail against the 'elites', by which they mean the bankers and politicians responsible for the financial crisis and its aftermath, and the wide range of experts that didn't see the crisis coming.

Across Europe, and not only in the eurozone, the populist left has set out an agenda targeted explicitly at the causes of the 2008 crash and the management of its effects. In doing so, it has sought either to capture or to open up space to the left of what had been, until recently, the dominant parties of European social democracy. In the UK, Jeremy Corbyn's Labour Party has launched a full-frontal assault on austerity and on the deregulation and greed upon which it lays the blame for the crisis. From the very beginning of his first leadership campaign in the summer of 2015, Corbyn has questioned the need for, and economic logic of, austerity. More than that, he has been explicit that the people suffering its consequences, namely the poor, the vulnerable, and public service workers in hospitals, schools and the police and fire services, were not responsible for the crisis and shouldn't be paying for its effects. He has attacked continued banker bonuses and has promised to increase taxes on the wealthy and corporations to pay for an increase in public expenditure to redress the obvious unfairness.

He has not been alone in making his case. In Portugal, the Left Bloc, led by Catarina Martins, which at the time of writing was in a coalition government in Lisbon with António Costa's Socialists, the Portuguese Communist Party and the Greens, has made a similar case. Martins ascribes the increased popularity of the Left Bloc in recent years to its explicit calls for an end to austerity. This message, delivered in the lee of Europe's severest economic and social crisis for decades, has given the Portuguese far left a share of power for the first time since the revolution of 1973 toppled the dictatorship of António de Oliveira Salazar.

In Spain, the leader of Podemos, Pablo Iglesias Turrión, drew huge crowds in the 2015 election campaign with his own confident anti-austerity message. Although Podemos came third in that election, it secured more than 20 per cent of the vote despite not having existed just two years earlier. It lost a little ground in the 2016 election, but still polled 21 per

cent of the popular vote, only 1 per cent less than the Socialists, and won seventy-one seats in the 350-seat parliament. It
remains an important new force in Spanish politics and may
yet come to play a significant role in the future direction of
the country. The anti-austerity message was also the one that
got Alexis Tsipras elected as Prime Minister in Greece, at
the head of the left-wing Syriza movement, in 2015, though
in his case the combined weight of the eurozone's economic
orthodoxy and Greece's need for international assistance
meant the government was subsequently forced to implement austerity in return for bail-outs.

It is not only in their attack on austerity and the 'elites'
where the populists of right and left tend to agree. In their
pitch to those left behind, both articulate a faith in the state's
ability to act in effective ways to address the concerns of
citizens. When selling their message to the voters, their
promise is that they will pull the levers of power at national
level, levers that mainstream politicians have had access to
for a long time, so the argument goes, but have been too
timid to pull. In reality, those levers may no longer exist
in the way they once did, and the promise may therefore
be hollow, but it nonetheless is a core populist claim that
state-level action can and will afford citizens a measure of
protection from the globalisation and technological change
that is whipping up a storm of economic insecurity. It is a
message that European voters have responded to.

And direct attacks on the EU itself have also been evident on both the far right and far left. The European Leadership Network, a London-based think-tank and advocacy organisation that draws together senior political, military and diplomatic figures from across Europe, conducted a review of eight of the main populist parties' attitudes to the EU and to the single currency in 2014.[31] Among the movements reviewed were UKIP in the UK, the Front National (FN) in France, Syriza in Greece, the Party for Freedom (PVV) in the Netherlands, the Danish People's Party (DPP), the Freedom Party of Austria (FPÖ), the Five Star Movement (M5S) in Italy and Jobbik in Hungary. The key similarity found between all the parties was their distrust and open criticism of the European Union. In fact, all of the reviewed parties advocated either exit from the Union, or radical changes to EU policies and/or a significant shifting of decision-making authority away from Brussels to national legislative bodies. While the study showed that only UKIP and the PVV favoured departure from the EU altogether, the other parties were all heavily Eurosceptic. The position of the DPP was typical. It opposed the introduction of what it called a 'European political union' and argued that Denmark should remain a sovereign state. Jobbik's argument was that Hungary's membership of the EU had damaged the country's economy and as a consequence the party favoured a referendum on amending Hungary's EU Accession Treaty.

The FN argued for reduced 'supranational' powers for the EU. Its leader, Marine Le Pen, claimed that it was, and still is, the 'duty of patriots to vote against Brussels'. Her attitude found echoes in the positions of the FPÖ and the M5S. Syriza, while not calling for a Greek exit from the EU, was scathing about what it saw as the latter's slavish adherence to neo-liberal economic orthodoxy, while Greece was forced to implement it.

In a demonstration of the populists' modus operandi, detailed ideas on how the EU should be radically reformed were few and far between. However, four of the reviewed parties, namely the FN, the PVV, Jobbik and the M5S, supported a reversion to trade agreements between countries in Europe that would only serve what they called 'national interests' and these agreements, by implication, would be blended with some sort of protectionism. Not for them the benefits of the single European market.

The FN and the PVV also supported outright withdrawal from the euro as a common currency. The FPÖ, while not going that far, stated that the party would not oppose a negotiated break-up or restructuring of the euro, possibly into northern and southern European variants, and the M5S's position was to call for a referendum on continued Italian membership of the euro. Three of the other parties reviewed (UKIP, Jobbik and the DPP) operate in countries that have never adopted the euro (respectively the UK, Hungary and

Denmark) but of course strongly opposed any thought of one day entering it.

Where the right parts company with the left, and where it seeks to capitalise on other elements of the crisis facing the EU, is on matters of immigration and security. The message on immigration is unrelentingly tough. Not only do the right-wing populists believe in the power of the state but they believe in the power of 'their' state. They have sought to mobilise support around both what they say are the negative economic effects of immigration, especially for those at the lower end of the pay scale, and what they describe as a developing threat to national culture and identity. The evidence for their economic claims is dubious at best and in many cases, just plain wrong. But that doesn't stop them making the case or the case being heard by those who want to hear it.

In Germany, Frauke Petry, previously a co-leader of Alternative für Deutschland, has openly admitted that the migration crisis of 2015 was the launch pad for her party's success. In her desire to demonstrate just how tough she is on immigration, at the height of the controversy over the large flows of refugees and migrants into Germany in 2015 she even suggested that it might be necessary to shoot migrants at the border. More latterly, as an AfD leader interested in trying to broaden her appeal, she tried to make a distinction between asylum seekers and economic migrants, arguing that Germany does indeed need to make room for some of the former and less of the latter. Her criticism of Angela Merkel's government was that it had stopped making a meaningful distinction between the two.

When the EU–Turkey deal on the management of the migrant crisis significantly reduced the flow to Germany, Petry then pivoted to a different but related argument, namely that the government needed to act to prevent the developing 'Islamification' of Germany. To make her case, she argued that migrants were responsible for a rise in cases of sexual harassment, for changes to school practices involving the introduction of separate swimming classes for boys and girls, and for the destruction of Christian prayer rooms in hostels used by asylum seekers.

This concern over Islamification is a recurring theme on the European populist right. It has been a notable strand of thinking in the far-right Sweden Democrats, the FN, the FPÖ and the PVV, and across much of central and eastern Europe. In Hungary, it is a core theme of the Prime Minister, Viktor Orbán. Orbán, in fact, goes even further. He draws an explicit and direct line between the influx of Muslim migrants and refugees to Europe and terrorism, and argues that large-scale Muslim migration into Europe is a threat to both Europe's physical security and to the integrity of European civilisation.

In making all these arguments, the parties of the populist

right and left have, as Steve Richards has argued, been aided and abetted by the weaknesses of mainstream political parties in Europe. The mainstream left has been unable or unwilling to articulate a case for what the state can and should do to assuage peoples' fears and to manage their insecurities. Most of its leaders cut their political teeth in an environment where promising a bigger role for the state spelt electoral disaster. The mainstream right, meanwhile, has for the most part not even tried. By ideological predisposition, it prefers small government and is clinging to this view, despite mounting evidence that people are crying out for government action. Mainstream parties of both left and right have also failed to conduct a serious conversation with their own voters on the need for, and costs and benefits of, immigration. For long periods, either the issue was ignored, or outlandish claims were made about how it would be controlled, only for those promises to go blatantly unfulfilled.

The lack of answers emanating from both the mainstream right and left, and the reluctance of many of the leaders of both to break with the old economic and political orthodoxies of the past, has played directly into the hands of the populists. In the referendum on UK membership of the EU, for example, and as we will see in the next chapter, the Remain campaign allowed itself to be positioned as the party of the status quo and of the elite in a country agitating for change. It lacked a future vision of Britain in which membership of a reformed European Union would play an integral part. The lack of answers in the mainstream has also masked the real weaknesses within and among the populists themselves. Beppe Grillo's Five Star Movement in Italy, for example, runs on virtually no policy and on an anti-politics sentiment. Where it has won power locally, such as in elections for the mayoralty in Rome in June 2016, it has performed extremely poorly. Within months of winning there, the administration of Five Star's Virginia Raggi was mired in a corruption scandal and several members of her cabinet had resigned. She has stumbled from one crisis to another ever since. Five Star ought to be comfortably beatable if mainstream Italian parties could figure out what kind of alternative future is both desirable and deliverable in a country that has experienced almost no economic growth for a decade. In Germany, the far-right Alternative für Deutschland has often seemed close to falling apart under the weight of its own internal divisions. These are profound, with one wing of the party being more moderate and interested in taking a pragmatic approach to policy in order to build broader appeal, and another wing being more nationalist and xenophobic. This did begin to take its effect on poll ratings but as the result of the September 2017 elections to the Bundestag showed, in which the AfD secured ninety-four seats, the effect of the AfD's rhetoric has already changed German and European politics and has scared

Angela Merkel's Christian Democratic Union into changing its policy towards refugees entering the country.

The behaviour of the EU and some of its leaders should also not escape examination in this context. The mismanagement of the euro crisis through a combination of failure to restructure banks and sovereign debt while foisting the cost of bail-outs on to taxpayers, and then subjecting them to austerity, must be seen as central. This is not only because of the economic and social pain this caused, which the populists have been able to exploit. It is because at the heart of the 'no alternative' mantra on the economy has been the insistence that in return for economic assistance from one's European partners a state must follow a particular set of social and economic policy prescriptions, irrespective of the views and wishes of the voters. The claim, peddled at length by the populists, that at the heart of the European project, and in particular at the heart of the eurozone, there exists a group of unelected economic technocrats who will brook no opposition from a leader with a democratic mandate, has merit. In Greece the troika has been described as acting like a second legislative body, and in both Spain and Italy the European institutions have at times effectively overruled national governments and threatened them to get their way.

It is not a coincidence that a central element of the platform of many populist parties in Europe is the claim that the EU is an anti-democratic entity defending the interests of the political and business elite and not the interests of ordinary citizens. Unless the leaders of the EU find a more effective way not just of countering this argument rhetorically, but of allowing the increased economic flexibility necessary to ensure national democratic politics remains meaningful, the entire European integration project will remain vulnerable. Whether this is done or not, what cannot be escaped is the conclusion that the populists have been able to thrive by focusing on, and claiming to have solutions for, the real and deep-seated problems that Europe faces and that have been described in the opening chapters of this book. The populists' apparent solutions may be dubious, and in some cases they are almost certainly a cruel form of political fantasy. On the far right especially, they are downright dangerous. But it is the approach of much of the incumbent leadership in Europe and alongside that the mainstream parties' failure to acknowledge for most of the last decade the scale of the crisis being inflicted on people that forms the platform for their success. Some of the populist leaders have sought to exacerbate Europe's challenges and in that sense, they are not only bereft of solutions but are themselves now an important part of the problem. But they are also primarily the symptom and not the cause. Nowhere demonstrates that more clearly, perhaps, than the UK's vote on Brexit.

CHAPTER 4

BREXIT

At 4.40 on the morning of 24 June 2016 the BBC announced to a stunned world that the UK had voted to leave the European Union. Voters had been warned their economy would collapse, the life-chances of their children would be constrained, and their country would be less safe in such an eventuality, but they went ahead and voted for it anyway.[32] In looking for reasons why, there are many in Europe who are hoping beyond hope that this was a specifically British phenomenon: a vote by a country that has never fully come to terms with its place in Europe, expressing its island mentality and opting to go its own way. That they choose to believe this is understandable, since to believe anything else might suggest Brexit is a harbinger of the disintegration of the European Union itself. Emmanuel Macron's victory over Marine Le Pen in 2017 gave them succour, as did the failure of the Party for Freedom, led by Geert Wilders, to win the national election in the Netherlands. As

argued in the last chapter, however, relief may be prema-
ture. The Eurosceptic populist movements scattered around
the EU have put down deep roots. They may yet come to
enjoy a breakthrough elsewhere. And while the decision of
the British public to vote for Brexit may have had powerful
local drivers, it was also influenced in important respects
by the Leave campaign's ability to use the EU's own failures
and weaknesses against it. Both the UK-specific and wider
European aspects of the campaign, and the interplay between them, need to be understood to judge what Brexit's
significance might ultimately be for the European project as
a whole.

BREXIT: MADE IN BRITAIN

It is possible to place the blame for Brexit, if one thinks blame
needs to be apportioned, on to just one man. The open question is which man it should be. For some, David Cameron is
the culprit. His critics argue that here was a Prime Minister
who had consistently put Conservative Party interest above
the national interest. In doing so, he had exercised appalling
judgement, taken a huge gamble with the country's future,
and lost.[33] Given the scale of the consequences, which even
now are difficult to fully discern, he must therefore go down
as the worst Prime Minister in decades. Others turn their
ire not on Cameron but on Boris Johnson. He, it is claimed,
neither truly believes in Brexit nor expected the Leave side

to win. He therefore felt able to sit centre stage in a national drama with a view only to boosting his own chances of one day leading the Conservative Party. His effectiveness in campaigning for Leave, along with that of his cabinet colleague Michael Gove, is seen as all the more unforgivable in light of what are assumed to be his dubious motives.[34]

Then there are those who believe the blame should be focused not on the Conservative Party at all, but on Labour. It was Tony Blair, after all, who encouraged a major enlargement of the EU to the east, underestimated the scale of subsequent eastern European migration to Britain, and then failed to impose transitional controls to deal with it. He is said to have undermined public trust both in the EU and in the immigration system in Britain as a result.[35] His decision to join in the US-led invasion of Iraq in 2003 is further seen as relevant since, so the argument goes, it massively destabilised the Middle East and helped unleash the chaos and the politically very contentious flows of migrants into Europe from the south. Blair's critics also note that he had form with regard to breaking promises to give voters a direct say on what the future of the UK's relationship with Europe ought to be. He indicated he would back a referendum on the new EU constitution before the 2005 election, only to pull back from that commitment when the constitution was renamed the Lisbon Treaty soon after it. But just as with Cameron on the Tory side of the fence, Blair isn't the only Labour leader to take the heat on Brexit. Jeremy Corbyn, a politician with a history of Euroscepticism, has also been accused by many of not even trying to win the referendum, when it came, for Remain.[36]

All of these critiques of Britain's leading political figures with regard to Brexit have some merit. Cameron certainly did put Conservative Party interests first, not only in calling the referendum in the first place, which was done to placate hard-line Brexit supporters in his party, but at points during the campaign too. According to a number of accounts of the short campaign, and because Cameron assumed he was going to win, he held back from attacking Johnson, Gove and other Tory Leave campaigners as energetically as he otherwise might have done. He did this to improve his chances of preserving Tory unity after referendum success.[37] Blair's mistakes, too, are clear in hindsight. Immigration from eastern Europe *was* underestimated. Before the Labour government left office that error was acknowledged. As everyone now knows, and most accept, the invasion of Iraq also took place on a false prospectus and the post-invasion story of that country has been anything but happy. There are more than a few who draw a direct line from the decision to topple Saddam Hussein and the subsequent rise of Islamic State.[38] And as for Jeremy Corbyn, the only surprise is perhaps that he summoned up as much muted enthusiasm for Remain as he did. The Jeremy Corbyn who campaigned in such a lacklustre manner in the 2016 Brexit referendum certainly bore little resemblance to the man who fought such an impressive general election campaign twelve months later. Of the four leadership figures discussed here, Johnson is perhaps the hardest one upon whom to pass judgement. He certainly sat on the fence on the issue of Brexit long enough to make questions about where the subsequent force and energy of his campaign performance came from legitimate. But without a window on to the man's soul, who but he can know for sure what was driving his actions?

All that said, the specific case against each of these individuals also suffers from important limitations. Yes, had Corbyn fought harder, he might have delivered enough Labour voters to make the difference for Remain, but that is far from certain. Had Cameron exhibited less hubris and complacency, the result might have been different, but which party leader worth his or her salt wouldn't have had one eye on the stability of the party while also trying to deliver what was thought best for the country? The mistakes of the Blair administration certainly contributed to the context within which the referendum eventually took place but by the time of the referendum, Blair had been out of office for nine years. And while the disintegration of Iraq has had regional consequences, can anyone really blame the decision to invade that country for the totality of the turmoil unleashed by the Arab Spring, and for the failure of the West to do more to stop the war in Syria? And what of the other drivers of the migration that figured so prominently in the campaign? The gut-wrenching poverty blighting lives from central Asia to sub-Saharan Africa, or the demographic time bomb in the region upon which much of the flow of refugees and migrants now rests? And though Boris Johnson can claim credit for adding intellectual heft and star quality to the Brexit campaign, is it not also the case that he and his colleagues in Leave were the beneficiaries of ground made fertile over a long period by others in the UK and by events elsewhere in Europe?

The role of Nigel Farage, whatever one thinks of him, should not be underestimated. Farage has limited reach within the British electorate. He is loved by some, but hated by many more, and has failed to be elected to Parliament despite seven attempts. That said, it is also true that he took his United Kingdom Independence Party (UKIP) from nowhere to second place in the European elections in 2009 with 16.5 per cent of the vote. He harried David Cameron as leader of the opposition continuously, taking votes from the Tories on the right and threatening to take more. In the European elections in May 2014, UKIP topped the poll, with a staggering 26.6 per cent of the vote. Two Conservative MPs, Douglas Carswell and Mark Reckless, were persuaded to defect to UKIP in the months after that victory. Farage was also able to reach beyond the patriotic Tory right, deep into working-class Labour heartlands with a message that Labour had sold working-class voters out and become part of an establishment that was the problem, not the solution.[39]

The strategic significance of Farage's progress was not in any total UKIP breakthrough, but as with populists elsewhere in Europe, in his ability to dictate the terms of debate and to force changes to the positions of others. Right from the start, Cameron was acutely aware of the power of UKIP's message among Eurosceptic Conservative members of Parliament and the Tory rank and file. He was constantly upping the ante with an increasingly Eurosceptic tone of his own precisely to manage the problem. To help him in his effort to win the leadership of the Conservative Party in the first place, he had promised to pull the party out of the European People's Party, the centre-right grouping in the European Parliament that many Eurosceptic Tories considered to be too federalist and pro-EU. In September 2007, he gave a 'cast iron guarantee' that if he became Prime Minister, he would hold a referendum on the Lisbon Treaty. He subsequently reneged on that promise in November 2009, arguing that it was no longer necessary since the Lisbon Treaty had already been ratified. It was a decision that left him open to accusations of betrayal and that frequently came back to haunt him. He was constantly under pressure thereafter to prove his Eurosceptic credentials.

He tried to replace his commitment to a referendum on

the treaty with a commitment to a 'referendum lock', a declaration that a referendum would automatically follow any future further transfer of power to Brussels.[40] In December 2011, and again under massive pressure from the Eurosceptic wing of the Conservative Party, Cameron stood alone at a Brussels summit at which all other member states agreed to proceed with an agreement that later became known as the Fiscal Compact.[41] In January 2013, in a speech delivered at the offices of Bloomberg in London and with UKIP continuing to ride high in the polls, he went further and made the fateful promise that he would get fundamental reform of the European Union and then call an in/out referendum on Britain's membership. He said:

> The next Conservative manifesto will ask for a mandate from the British people for a Conservative government to negotiate a new settlement with our European partners ... and when we have negotiated that new settlement we will give the British people a referendum with a very simple in-or-out choice: to stay in the EU on these new terms or come out altogether.[42]

Just weeks before UKIP's triumph in the 2014 European elections, he went further again, outlining in an article for the *Sunday Telegraph* the areas where he wanted to see reform of the European Union. These included:

Powers flowing away from Brussels, not always to it ... Businesses liberated from red tape and benefiting from the strength of the EU's own market – the biggest and wealthiest on the planet – to open up greater free trade with North America and Asia.[43] Our police forces and justice systems able to protect British citizens unencumbered by unnecessary interference from the European institutions ... Free movement to take up work, not free benefits ... new mechanisms in place to prevent vast migrations across the continent. And dealing properly with the concept of 'ever closer union', enshrined in the treaty ... It may appeal to some countries. But it is not right for Britain, and we must ensure we are no longer subject to it.[44]

The expressed concerns over free movement to take up benefits, and the reference to 'vast migrations across the continent', presaged a series of attempts by Cameron and his team to address the question of immigration. In a speech to the Conservative Party conference in October 2014 the then Prime Minister offered a statement of intent on the question of free movement within the European Union that left no subsequent room for obfuscation. 'Britain,' he said, 'I know you want this sorted so I will go to Brussels, I will not take no for an answer and – when it comes to free movement – I will get what Britain needs.'[45] Press reports in the same month suggested he was considering a new annual cap on the numbers of low-skilled workers from other parts of Europe who were allowed to enter the UK. This was publicly dismissed by Angela Merkel within days. Cameron's team then moved on to consider an 'emergency brake' on numbers in certain circumstances. Amid internal rows between civil servants and Cameron's special advisers, this was also dropped in the final hours before a speech delivered at the offices of the JCB manufacturing group on 28 November, to be replaced with a ban on in-work benefits for EU migrants until they had worked and contributed to the system for four years.[46]

Ultimately, the problem for Cameron was that while he ratcheted up the rhetoric to manage his own party and the threat from Nigel Farage, he both contributed to a prevailing mood of Euroscepticism in the country and set public expectations that his subsequent negotiating position in relation to the EU utterly failed to meet. He vacillated between a hard-line political position on the one hand and a more pragmatic diplomatic stance on the other. His political instincts were to demand more radical change from other EU leaders, but he allowed himself to be reined in by civil service advisers, sometimes against the wishes of members of his own senior political team.[47]

The deal Cameron struck with the EU, when it came, was a pale shadow of what he had promised. He wanted a thirteen-year emergency brake that would mean any new

EU workers arriving in that time frame would be excluded from in-work benefits for four years. He wanted a ban on the rights of EU workers to send child benefits home. And he wanted a commitment that neither future references to ever-closer union, nor any measures taken to deepen monetary union in future EU treaties, would apply to the UK. What he got on in-work benefits was an emergency brake of only seven years and not an exclusion on EU worker access to benefits for four years but an agreement that access to such benefits would be gradually phased in over four years. He did not get his ban on child benefit being exported but only a more modest commitment that child benefits exported could be linked to the cost of living in the country where the child was living. The French pushed back exceptionally hard on the issue of what rules applied to EU members outside the eurozone, smelling a British ruse to undercut the single market. The only real area where Cameron got what he wanted in full was on the written recognition received that the UK was not committed to ever-closer union.[48]

Diplomatically, Cameron ran up against strong opposition from some of the countries the UK often counted as allies in internal EU debates. Eastern European states in particular were against what he was proposing on changes to the benefits system since many of their own citizens would be the ones negatively affected. The V4 group of countries (Poland, Hungary, the Czech Republic and Slovakia) worked together to impede the British government's ambitions.[49] Not only did the modest reforms that were agreed with European partners do little to satisfy Eurosceptic opinion both among members of the public and in the media, but the fact that Cameron had clearly tried hard and failed was itself deeply damaging, not only to him personally but to support for UK membership of the Union. Nothing seemed to demonstrate more clearly that even a democratically elected Prime Minister had little influence when faced with the already agreed rules and commitments of the European Union. There is no doubt that this optic contributed to the ultimate referendum defeat.

Other factors, though, were also crucial. One of them, as Tim Shipman's brilliant book *All Out War* makes clear, was the creation, in June 2015, of Conservatives for Britain.[50] Led by Steve Baker, this group of Conservative MPs did much between the time of its formation and the onset of the short referendum campaign in late February 2016 to shape the terrain of the referendum battle in ways profoundly helpful to the Leave campaign. For a start, the group was instrumental in changing the referendum question that was eventually put to the British people. The government had wanted the question to be: 'Should the United Kingdom remain a member of the European Union?' This worried Baker and his colleagues because propositions couched as a choice between Yes and No were perceived to heavily favour those on the

Yes side of the campaign. A concerted campaign by Baker and his colleagues persuaded the Electoral Commission to change the question to: 'Should the UK remain a member of the European Union or leave the European Union?' ICM polling suggested that this change alone might have added as much as 4 per cent to the Leave vote.

The Conservatives for Britain group also won a key battle over the rules governing civil service behaviour during the campaign. Under normal rules in the UK, a period of 'purdah' applies in which civil servants are unable to do anything that may influence an election result once the formal campaign period has started. Cameron's team had sneakily included a clause in the Referendum Bill that would have scrapped purdah in this case, allowing the full weight of the government machine to churn out what would have been, in the eyes of the Leave campaign, a constant stream of pro-Remain messages. The government's rationale was that Britain's interaction with the EU required the civil service to continue functioning as normal or the process of government itself would grind to a halt. After a battle that was to last through the summer and autumn of 2015, however, the government eventually lost the deciding vote in the House of Commons by 312 to 285 votes. Purdah was reinstated.

These victories, along with the Conservative Party defeat of a Labour and Liberal Democrat attempt to lower the voting age for the referendum to sixteen, as in the referendum on

Scottish independence, were clearly influential in determining the referendum outcome. The Leave campaign certainly had its divisions and problems, but after some brutal infighting, these were effectively overcome and these early victories for a key group of Brexit supporters helped to set the scene for what would later be a winning campaign.

Things were more complicated on the Remain side. For one thing, the campaign needed to be cross-party, which meant at the heart of the entire enterprise sat the delicate task of bringing together people who would normally be sworn political enemies. According to accounts of some of those who were involved, this seems to have been accomplished well, after initial hesitancy on the part of Cameron's advisers in No. 10.[51] What turned out to be the more difficult task, however, and ultimately the more significant in terms of its effect on the referendum campaign and its outcome, was not the challenge of inter-party relations but that of intra-party management.

The divisions in the Conservative Party were so great that Cameron was forced to agree that the party itself, in terms of its campaign machinery, fundraising ability and canvassing data, could not be used for the purposes of fighting the campaign. Under pressure of threats of ministerial resignations, he was also forced to allow cabinet members to campaign for Leave, against an 'agreed government position', without a requirement to resign their posts. This, coupled with the reluctance to launch 'blue on blue' attacks on Conservative Brexiteers for fear of tearing the Tory Party apart in the process, typified the sense in which Cameron was forced to fight the campaign with one hand tied behind his back. Things were only marginally less complex on the Labour side of the equation. As already noted, the Labour leader was a long-time Eurosceptic who appeared to have been dragged into a lethargic willingness to campaign for Remain only under pressure from the vast majority of the members of his own parliamentary party. While many moderate Labour advisers were in leading positions in the official Britain Stronger in Europe campaign, moreover, the party itself officially decided to set up its own Labour In for Britain vehicle.[52] The party had been badly scarred by the experience of campaigning alongside David Cameron and the Chancellor, George Osborne, in the Scottish referendum in 2014. It blamed much of its subsequent wipe-out in Scotland at the hands of the Scottish National Party (SNP) in the 2015 general election on that experience, and was clear it intended no repeat. This was an especially acute concern given the way UKIP was eating into the Labour vote in some northern and coastal English constituencies. In the local elections, just six weeks prior to the referendum itself, Labour had suffered the worst set of results of any opposition party since 1992. It was in a weak position and couldn't afford to be seen as in cahoots with Cameron and Osborne.

It was in this mix of conditions, with the Tory party machinery side-lined, the cabinet split, the Labour leader lukewarm, and his party half in the designated Remain campaign and half out so it could maintain some semblance of independence, that the short referendum campaign was fought. Amid concern that Labour would not be able to get its share of the Remain vote to the polls, Cameron and Osborne also appear to have been less aware than they might have been of their own limited appeal in the relevant constituencies and communities in northern England.

The content of Remain campaign messages was also not what it might have been. In particular, what became known as 'project fear' seemed to backfire. As the Remain campaign piled on warnings of the economic pain that would follow a Brexit vote, and mobilised the Treasury, many leading economists, a large number of business leaders and international figures such as Barack Obama to deliver the message, many voters discounted it because they no longer trusted those delivering it.[53] The Remain campaign appeared as the defence of a status quo that many voters felt unhappy with. There also appeared to be an inconsistency at the heart of the campaign. On the one hand, the message was that Brexit would be a huge leap into the unknown. On the other, Osborne had the Treasury pumping out precise figures, to the effect that Brexit would cost every family in the country £4,300.

There is no doubt that all of this was impactful on the

outcome of the referendum. But still it is an account that captures more of the colour and personality of those most closely involved, the tactics they deployed and the constraints they laboured under than it is an account speaking to the bigger historical and longer-term context in which the referendum took place. More than one observer and combatant in the referendum has justifiably commented on the fact that no Remain campaign over a few short weeks and months could have reversed the intense Euroscepticism in Britain's press and parts of its political establishment that had been allowed to build up over several decades. And as the former Labour Europe minister Denis MacShane has pointed out, Britain was unique in Europe in that it had never had, during the entire period of its membership of the EU, a sustained period in which both main political parties were positive in their attitude towards the European project.[54]

British Euroscepticism is, in fact, deep rooted. It is also often based on a deeply ideological interpretation of what the EU is and what it stands for, not so much in terms of identity politics and an approach to international relations but in terms of sovereignty and political economy. For much of the first four decades after the end of World War Two, the Labour Party was hostile to Europe, seeing in it a vehicle for stripping a British government of the power to shape a radically different political economy at home. Attitudes changed in the early 1990s and in the Blair–Brown years Labour was much more pro-European. Some in the party have, however, remained sceptical throughout. Jeremy Corbyn is one of them. His first campaign to be leader of the Labour Party in 2015 offers an illustration. When pushed to articulate his position on Europe, he couched it entirely in terms of political economy. He refused to rule out voting No to the UK's continued membership of the EU in the impending referendum. In doing so, he attacked the EU for its allowance of tax havens in places like Monaco. He focused not on the EU's role in changing the structure of European relations and in saving Europe from its calamitous and conflictual past, but almost entirely on the kind of deal that Cameron might get from his renegotiation with EU partners instead. He demanded that the EU end austerity, provide more workers' rights and environmental protections, and end the race to the bottom in corporation tax rate cuts among member states, and he feared that the new deal Cameron would put to the country would be a deal that negotiated such protections away.[55] There was no indication from Corbyn that he viewed British membership of the EU as strategically significant in an increasingly dangerous and unstable world, or indeed that in the age of globalisation, his own domestic political economy goals could only really be achieved if Britain were part of such a bloc. His approach was transactional with regard to what the EU could offer his own domestic project.

If it could be persuaded to turn to the left in its management of the economy and society, he was in. If not, he was out.

On the right too, this tendency has been evident for decades. Recall Margaret Thatcher's famous speech in Bruges in 1988. 'We have not', she said, 'successfully rolled back the frontiers of the state in Britain, only to see them reimposed at European level with a European super-state exercising a new dominance from Brussels.'[56] The leading Brexiteers today still bristle with ideological fervour along both axes to which Thatcher referred. They yearn for what they see as Britain's national freedom, for the right of the country to make its own decisions, but there is also little doubt that what they want the freedom to do is to deregulate the British economy, to strip it of what they see as excessive social protections imposed by Europe, and to let the market rip.

BREXIT: MADE IN EUROPE

The backdrop to the referendum campaign was therefore not just one of flawed personalities providing inadequate leadership, nor of attempts to manage internal divisions in the Conservative Party. It was not Nigel Farage's triumph alone, nor the victory only of a well-organised group of Brexit supporters who knew how to prepare the ground. It was one of politically bipartisan, long-term ambivalence to the EU. This ambivalence was further fuelled by what seemed to be powerful evidence of the weaknesses and failures of the EU itself. Eurosceptic voices on both the left and right of British politics have regularly shaped their arguments by reference to the scale of the crisis facing the single currency and the inadequate, incompetent and unjust nature of ongoing efforts to manage it. As the eurozone nose-dived into the double-dip recession and, for some, depression described in Chapters 2 and 3 of this book, the right in Britain argued 'There but for the grace of God go we' while the left, particularly the hard left, looked on in horror at the way the repayment of private debt had been prioritised over taxpayer interests while deeply counter-productive austerity had been the result. As Britain's economy continued to grow, moreover, the juxtaposition with what was happening in Europe put wind in the sails of those arguing that Britain had nothing to learn about economics from the Europeans and that more consideration should be given to how far Britain could soar if only it were not burdened by the excesses of growth-killing EU rules. As the EU bail-outs for Greece were being agreed, those expressing disapproval of the UK's membership of the Union touched 60 per cent.

The eurozone crisis was also pivotal to the rise of UKIP and a key driver of the feverish Eurosceptic activity in the Conservative Party because it meant that as unemployment soared in Europe, tens of thousands of additional people travelled from other EU countries to Britain in search of work. This destroyed Cameron's earlier pledge to the public to get annual net immigration down to under 100,000 and it put rocket boosters under UKIP's claim that extra pressure was being piled on communities and their public services.[57] Net immigration to the UK increased from 177,000 in 2012 to 318,000 in 2014, helping to fuel the UKIP victory in the 2014 European elections.

Eurosceptic sentiment was also boosted by the EU's failing effort to manage the migration crisis. I will return to some of the deep divisions and intra-European hostility that characterised this in the next chapter but it was observable that as a million migrants arrived in Europe in 2015, an almost fourfold increase on the numbers from the year before, and with a huge migrant camp at Calais in France made up of people trying to get to the UK, support for Brexit leapt up. Angela Merkel's decision in September 2015 to declare that Germany was open to refugees, widely considered to have offered extra encouragement to migrants and to have sown deep discord within the EU, amplified the sentiment. Some polls showed that the migrant crisis throughout the summer and autumn of 2015 had added 5 per cent to levels of support for Brexit. So worried about another wave of migration in 2016 was David Cameron that this consideration apparently weighed heavily in his decision to hold the referendum in June that year rather than to wait until 2017.

At the height of Cameron's attempt at renegotiation, the inherent difficulties of securing reform inside the EU were also made abundantly apparent. Martin Schulz, then president of the European Parliament, refused to guarantee that the parliament would not seek to amend, after the event, any deal Cameron did agree with other European leaders, a claim that enabled Leave supporters to argue that even the paltry deal Cameron subsequently secured could not be seen as legally binding. The whole negotiation process also seemed emblematic of a deep inflexibility on what EU membership meant and was allowed to mean.

If one wishes to understand where the content of the Leave campaign came from, therefore, one need look little further than to this list of perceived weaknesses in the European Union itself. The Leave campaign slogan, 'Take Back Control', was a laser-guided missile carrying the message that Britain had given up its sovereignty on the one hand to a group of other elected leaders who were uninterested in reform or in responding to Britain's needs and to a bunch of unelected bureaucrats in Brussels on the other. In that framing, the Leave campaign asked: what was the point in electing your own Prime Minister at home if membership of the European Union rendered him or her powerless? And what was the point of democracy at all if the important decisions had been taken out of the reach of the British ballot box? Their case was readily recognisable by many of those who had been subjected to the troika treatment in Greece, but also to the indignity of seeing Prime Ministers in Italy and Spain being effectively told what to do by Jean-Claude Trichet in his time at the helm of the European Central Bank.

The poor performance of the European economy over the last decade when compared to the UK economy, at least in terms of overall growth, was also used as a platform to make the case that the UK would be better off outside. Europe, it was claimed by Leave campaigners, represented the stagnating heart of the past. The world outside Europe, a world of rapidly growing emerging economies, was the future. The near-calamitous collapse of the single currency was used as evidence that the UK had had a lucky escape in not joining the euro some years earlier, but also in making the case that the trajectory of ever-closer union upon which all EU members were said to be set would inevitably end in failure. And the mismanagement of the economy in Greece, Spain and Italy was used as ammunition to demonstrate that the UK could not afford to have its destiny tied to incompetent, and in some cases corrupt, governments in other parts of Europe that couldn't be trusted.

Issue can be taken with many of these lines of attack, but that doesn't mean they lacked or still lack political effectiveness. On balance, it can be argued that the Brexit vote happened for all kinds of reasons specific to Britain, some of them short-term, some more deeply ingrained. But it can also be argued that what fuelled the Leave campaign so successfully in the years leading up to 23 June 2016 was the very visible struggle the EU itself was having to persuasively demonstrate both its legitimacy and its effectiveness. In that sense, the forces of Euroscepticism elsewhere on the continent know what playbook to use even if they also know they need to adapt it to their own circumstances. They need the EU to fail. The question of whether Brexit ultimately sparks contagion will also therefore be decided not only by how effective and skilful Eurosceptic political movements are in the years ahead but by how effective the EU is at managing its weaknesses and overcoming its failures. A single currency capable of withstanding crises is absolutely central. Inclusive and widespread economic growth matters. Effective collective management of the migration challenge is inextricably linked to the EU's prospects of survival. Demonstrating that membership of the Union makes citizens safer, not less safe, is core to the entire project's legitimacy. And finding the wherewithal to show that EU membership is compatible with unique national aspirations and preferences will most likely be decisive. Can the EU deliver any or all of these things and to what extent has it used the experience of crisis to show it is really trying? It is to these questions that I turn next.

CHAPTER 5

CRISIS MANAGEMENT

I n the first four chapters of this book, I have outlined what I see as the multidimensional nature of the crisis facing the EU today and the combination of external threats and internal weaknesses that have left it vulnerable. I turn next to an examination and evaluation of the EU's efforts to respond. On monetary union, new strategies to meet security threats and the challenge of migration, the EU has been active on all the issues that matter. The question of central importance now is whether these reform efforts have been enough.

At the heart of recent EU activism has been the effort to stabilise the single currency. In the midst of several member states being driven to the point of insolvency, eurozone leaders did find the will to provide bail-outs to countries and banks on the front line. Both where the money ultimately went and the conditions attached to it were hugely controversial, as discussed elsewhere in this book, but four of the countries accepting support, namely Cyprus, Ireland,

Portugal and Spain, exited their bail-out programmes and returned to borrowing on international markets without the need for programme extensions. Many of the crisis countries showed themselves willing to take the most drastic measures to stay in the single currency. The pain inflicted was compounded by the fact that most of it landed on those least able to bear it, but the measures taken nonetheless demonstrated what some would see as an impressive determination by several governments to do whatever was necessary to maintain national membership of the euro. For its part, the European Central Bank, once under Mario Draghi's leadership, played a pivotal role in ending the immediate crisis of 2010–12. Not only did Draghi's public commitment that the bank would do 'whatever it takes within its mandate' to save the single currency take the heat out of the euro crisis in July 2012, but since then the ECB's pursuit of a low interest rate policy has been vital.[58] Shortly after Draghi uttered his now famous words the ECB also announced the creation of a new monetary policy instrument to support sovereign bond markets in the eurozone, which helped take the pressure off several member states with still high debt-to-GDP ratios.

As the immediate crisis eased, eurozone leaders turned their efforts to reform of the euro's underlying institutional architecture and its governance arrangements. The Fiscal Compact, as noted earlier, was negotiated to bring discipline to eurozone public spending. This sought to prevent laxity and fraud of the kind experienced in Greece prior to 2009. The compact reinforces rules related to government deficits and debt levels and makes sanctions against those who break them automatic. Economic policy coordination across members is also now enhanced through the European Semester, an annual process designed to ensure that member states' economic and budgetary policies are aligned with objectives agreed at EU level. A European Stability Mechanism (ESM) has been set up to replace bilateral ad hoc loans to countries in distress with a sizeable, permanent facility that can borrow at low interest rates and lend to European countries that are solvent but may be struggling to gain access to the money markets. The ESM still comes with conditions, in the form of macro-economic adjustment programmes (another name for cuts, reforms to labour markets and other measures), but its existence should smooth the management of at least some future crisis scenarios.

Steps have also been taken to create a Banking Union. The Banking Union contains a Single Supervision Mechanism (SSM), designed to transfer authority for banking policy from national level to European level. This has the aim of preventing cosy national clubs of bankers, regulators and politicians from engaging in the kind of irresponsible behaviour that so damaged countries like Ireland and Spain prior to the last crisis. A second element, the Single Resolution Mechanism (SRM), has been designed as a more uniform pan-European procedure for dealing with failing banks across the eurozone. Technically, it is intended to make the resolution of failing banks more effective and to allow the application of common rules for such cases. Politically, its real significance is that it assumes a resolution procedure in which failing banks' creditors would be routinely bailed in while taxpayer bail-outs would in future be limited and very much the exception. The SRM is further backed by a Single Resolution Fund (SRF). This is supposed to gradually grow to €55 billion by 2024, paid for by a levy on the banks, and would be used to help recapitalise banks that had passed through the resolution procedure. Combined, these elements of the Banking Union amount to an attempt to break the doom loop between government finances and the finances of the banks. They are designed to make it more unlikely that a banking crisis will occur; to ensure that if one does occur the banks' creditors and not the taxpayer will pay the price; and that if taxpayer money is needed, not only is it limited in amount but it will come from a common European and not an isolated national source.

Alongside the Banking Union, Jean-Claude Juncker, the President of the European Commission, announced in 2014 that the EU would work to build a Capital Markets Union. This was a direct response to the belief that at the time of the last euro crisis European capital markets were not integrated enough and risk sharing across and between countries was too limited. The problem with this was that when the crisis came to a particular economy, everyone's assets and incomes there took a hammering, contributing to a downward spiral of tightening credit and falling investment and demand. If capital markets were more integrated across the eurozone, so the thinking goes, it ought to be possible to cushion the shock by providing investors and institutions with the ability to draw on relatively unaffected dividends, incomes and assets held elsewhere. This could smooth investment and demand even in a severe domestic crisis. The effects of any crisis that did occur could therefore be contained.

All of these proposals for the reform of the eurozone are to be welcomed. There is no doubt that in combination, the Fiscal Compact, the European Stability Mechanism, the Banking Union and the effort to create a Capital Markets Union amount to a serious effort to grapple with the weaknesses at the heart of the single currency. But are they enough? Unfortunately, it is hard to say with any confidence that they are.[59]

Major gaps in the effort to shore up the architecture of the euro remain. For one thing, the Banking Union remains incomplete. One problem concerns the way in which the SRM has been designed and is being implemented. Decisions over how and when to resolve a failing bank are, in practice, left exposed to extremely complex and inherently political decision-making processes, which means the rules are not being applied consistently. Politics often still trumps the diktats of sound finance. This is a danger especially when, for political reasons, a national government may not want to accept that a failing bank needs to be resolved rather than propped up with injections of taxpayer support. The Italian government has already had several run-ins with Brussels and the ECB in Frankfurt over precisely such issues.[60] Another major flaw is that the negotiations over the creation of a European Deposit Insurance Scheme are stalled. Germany, backed by Mario Draghi, wants lending institutions to cut their risks before any such scheme can start.[61] The status quo, in which supervision of the banks is carried out at European level but deposit insurance schemes remain national, is one in which national taxpayers could be left on the hook for what they perceive to be inappropriate European supervision decisions. This not only has the potential to stoke further political tension between eurozone institutions and national taxpayers in member states but it could create incentives inside member states to avoid or fail to facilitate appropriate bank supervision in the first place. Even more importantly, without a eurozone-wide scheme, national schemes paid for by national taxpayers will remain the only backstop behind the banks.

Since it also remains the case that, even with the better regulation now in place, the risk of systemic banking crises can never be totally eliminated, a further related weakness in eurozone reforms concerns the limited funds available to the Single Resolution Fund. Few believe the SRF would be sufficient to handle a systemic crisis affecting a large number of sizeable banking institutions. The question therefore remains as to whether the SRF itself has a backstop from a common eurozone taxpayer resource like the European Stability Mechanism, or whether it would be overwhelmed by the scale of bank failures in a crisis. Formally, an agreement to provide a common European backstop to the fund was agreed by eurozone finance ministers in 2013 but the details of what this would look like and how it would work in practice have not been set out. This leaves observers with the suspicion that the will to face a crisis collectively does not exist.

This is especially worrying because not enough is being done to tackle the eurozone systemic risk that remains. The former German finance minister Wolfgang Schäuble has warned that the quantitative easing practices of the ECB have stoked asset bubbles that may yet bring trouble, and that not enough is being done to address the problem of non-performing loans on the balance sheets of Europe's banks. Others note that concerns about excessive lending and borrowing in some parts of the eurozone, coupled to capital flows from surplus to deficit countries to facilitate them, have not gone away. There is also the not insignificant problem that some lending activity has been migrating from banks to non-banking institutions. This so-called shadow banking is largely outside effective regulatory control. There is a strong case for aggressive use of macro-prudential tools to address some of what is going on. These involve measures to restrict the behaviour of lenders, such as the imposition of higher minimum capital requirements on the banks; measures to restrict the behaviour of borrowers, such as ceilings on loan-to-value or debt-to-income ratios; and capital controls to restrict the cross-border flows that may be used to fuel an unsustainable boom. The problem is that such measures are not being applied aggressively enough.

A further complicating factor is that the use of tools such as capital controls is limited by the European Union Treaties and decisions over their use lie neither entirely with the ECB nor with the authorities inside the member states. European authorities can recommend measures and can warn about developing systemic risks but they cannot insist on action. The ECB also has authority, as part of the Single Supervision Mechanism, to address only the lending side of the equation. Tools aimed at influencing borrower behaviour are still left to national bodies, which may struggle to find the will to use them. This is especially true in current conditions where stagnating wages and living standards often drive demand for credit, while cutting off the supply of credit can be viewed as an attack on voters' aspirations. What all this means is that the euro is only as strong as its weakest link when it comes to prudential management of irresponsible financial behaviour and there are insufficient measures in place to prevent a crisis developing again.

Taking all of this together, two conclusions suggest themselves. First, a fresh banking crisis cannot be ruled out. Second, despite all the efforts at reform, the remaining weaknesses in the Banking Union suggest that if a crisis does occur, what has been done so far will be insufficient to prevent a return of the doom loop between the finances of the banks and the finances of their governments. The common thread in the failure to apply Single Resolution Mechanism rules consistently, the difficulty in agreeing a European Deposit Insurance Scheme and the failure to make clear there is a common European backstop behind the Single Resolution Fund is that of a reluctance on the part of national authorities to adopt genuinely European solutions. In the event of a crisis that affects systemically important banks, it will therefore still be national governments that have to make good on bank deposit guarantees. Bail-outs will still be required and it will be primarily national governments that are on the hook to provide them. To the extent that help from European institutions might be available, via the European Stability Mechanism, there is nothing to indicate that this would be automatic. In a crisis affecting some of the eurozone's largest economies, the ESM itself may be overwhelmed by the scale of the crisis. But whether it is or it isn't, the question of whether the rest of Europe is willing to stump up the required funds to help, and on what conditions, will be back on the agenda with a vengeance. With it will come the toxic politics that plagued relations between creditors and debtors in the last crisis.

Nor has the Capital Markets Union progressed to the point where the effects of any crisis might be smoothed. A recent study by the European Commission suggested that whereas over 80 per cent of asymmetric shocks are smoothed by integrated capital markets in the United States, which has much more integrated markets than Europe, between 50 and 70 per cent of such shocks are *not* smoothed in Europe.[62] The truth is that the different national capital markets that exist in the EU today are a complex product of history, politics and differing legal and regulatory systems. The creation of a Capital Markets Union is a process, not an event, and its completion could take decades.

That the eurozone is not out of the woods was clearly acknowledged in a major speech by President Macron in September 2017. The speech was reported for its ambitious reform agenda, and in particular for its proposal to create a greater degree of fiscal union, with a single European budget coming under the control of a European finance minister, answerable to the European Parliament. But more notable to this observer was that Macron and his team deemed it necessary to deliver such a speech in the first place and the candour with which it was delivered. 'Here we are', Macron said, 'with a Europe that is more fragile than ever.'[63] Here was the new President of the French Republic being as clear as possible that, far from being secure, the eurozone remains in peril. The period of growth being enjoyed in 2017/18 offers but a short window of opportunity to sort its remaining weaknesses out before it is buffeted and perhaps destroyed by another deep recession or crisis.

Elsewhere on the agenda, the EU has been reaching for solutions to its security challenges. Russia has loomed large, as one would expect. In the spring and summer of 2014, the EU rolled out a series of economic sanctions against Russia as a response to the latter's annexation of Crimea. Travel bans and asset freezes were introduced against 150 people and thirty-seven entities thought to be involved in actions against Ukraine's territorial integrity. To exploit Russia's perceived shortage of capital and investment, five major state-owned banks were also identified as core targets. EU nationals and companies were prohibited from buying or selling new Russian bonds or equity issued by any of them and loans to them were banned. Embargoes have been introduced on the export and import of arms and related material to and from Russia, along with embargoes on trade in dual-use goods (goods that may be used for both military and civilian purposes). And the export of certain energy-related equipment and technology has been restricted and made subject to specific prior authorisation by competent authorities in EU member states. The sanctions have been renewed a number of times since 2014 and will most likely not be lifted until the Minsk Agreement, negotiated by the leaders of Ukraine, Russia, Germany and France in February 2015, and which sets out a path to peace and restored territorial integrity for Ukraine, has been implemented. Beyond sanctions, the EU has been active in trying to counter Russian disinformation campaigns. For the last three years, an East Stratcom Task Force has been in operation, trying to raise awareness of Russian disinformation trends and practices, and to better explain EU policies in countries on the EU's eastern periphery where Russia is highly active. A new, more comprehensive strategy to deal with this threat is expected in 2018.

On counter-terrorism, the EU relegates itself to a secondary role, making clear that primary responsibility rests with member states. But in its secondary role, and since the shootings that took place in Paris in January 2015, the EU has acted to tighten firearms controls and has criminalised the training of terrorists, the facilitation of their travel and any attempts to fundraise for them. It has reinforced external border checks against pan-European databases and appointed a new EU commissioner for security, to help drive and implement the whole strategy. And it has acted to improve the exchange of information between member states via a European Counter Terrorism Centre. Europol has also been mandated to monitor and help member states to tackle online radicalisation.[64]

Perhaps the core of the EU's effort to address its own strategic vulnerabilities, however, comes in the area of defence. Since the Brexit vote, the defence ministers of Germany and France, backed by ministers from Italy and Spain, have tabled proposals to bring European military assets together more effectively, to spend more on defence, and to collaboratively develop technologies such as surveillance drones. They have talked of creating a joint EU civilian–military headquarters, to allow coordination of independent EU missions that entail both a military and a civilian component. Federica Mogherini, the EU's High Representative for Foreign Affairs and Security Policy, has also set out a process for EU member states to review and plan the future development of their militaries in line with the EU's overall needs and priorities. And the European Defence Agency has been tasked with working with member states to devise an integrated approach to developing the research, technology, skills and industrial base needed to underpin the required forces. At the sharp end, there is talk of strengthening EU rapid response forces, both to make them more relevant to current challenges and to make them more deployable.

Moves are also afoot to use a provision in the Lisbon Treaty to allow what is known as permanent structured cooperation (PESCO) among a sub-set of EU members. This could mean that some member states will make more binding commitments on defence cooperation. It is perhaps significant too that the European Commission has started to move into the defence space with its own European Defence Action Plan (EDAP). Commissioner Elżbieta Bieńkowska, who has responsibility for the EU's internal market, announced in early 2017 that for the first time EU budgets would be used to finance defence research projects. The sums indicated were small but the move is a new departure with potentially significant long-term consequences. The EDAP will fund research on disruptive technology, technologies where Europe is currently dependent on others, and areas where the EU currently suffers military capability gaps. Its goal is to stimulate the industrial base required to make the EU strategically autonomous.

Amid worries in some member states that what the EU is doing could undermine NATO, the body that binds the United States into the defence of Europe, the EU has been keen to describe its activism in this area as complementary to NATO rather than in competition with it. An EU–NATO Joint Declaration was signed at the NATO Warsaw summit in July 2016. This set out a range of security challenges facing both organisations and agreed that in future, NATO and the EU would collaborate to counter complex threats, tackle information warfare challenges and engage in more intelligence sharing. It was also agreed that operational co-operation would increase at sea and on migration, through increased sharing of maritime situational awareness data and the better coordination and mutual reinforcement of EU and NATO activities in the Mediterranean.

Despite all the activism, EU efforts to address defence and security concerns, like those aimed at strengthening the monetary union, leave much to be desired. While some Russian online troll farms are thought to number 400 people, the EU's East Stratcom Task Force has been made to do with fewer than fifteen staff. Many security experts have criticised its response as inadequate. Although the announced measures on improvements to counter-terrorism strategy are to be welcomed, there are still too many cases where information is not shared adequately or quickly enough, and this in a field where it is just about impossible to prevent every planned attack anyway. Defence cooperation should also be far more advanced than it is. The rationale for pursuing it is, after all, compelling. Many supporters of European integration believe that as Europe has deepened its economic and political ties, binding the interests and futures of individual European countries more closely together, it makes absolute sense for them to cooperate more on defence. They are right. The interests in common are formidable. Defending them collectively would be logical. But even were it not logical on these grounds, it would be on others. The European defence industry is embroiled in a slow-motion crisis. No individual member state of the EU can afford to invest the required amount in research and development to stay at the cutting edge of modern military technology. As that technology has become more sophisticated, the R&D costs have become so large that subsequent sales to a small national market alone cannot recoup the costs. It also has to be borne in mind that for much of the last decade, the US and EU28 have been cutting defence spending, while other emerging or re-emerging military powers have been radically increasing theirs (between 2005 and 2014 China increased defence spending by 167 per cent, Russia by 97 per cent, Saudi Arabia by 112 per cent and India by 39 per cent). Unless Europeans collaborate more with each other, several of their militaries will, in the not too distant future, find themselves using obsolete technology when compared to the world's best.

Another important element of the rationale for cooperation is the now constant pressure from the US for Europeans to share more of the military burden in NATO. As noted in Chapter 1, President Trump has on a number of occasions questioned continued US commitment to the defence of Europe unless the Europeans themselves step up to do more. He is not the first US leadership figure to pressure Europe in this area but the warnings are becoming increasingly blunt.

Nonetheless, achievements on EU defence cooperation have been patchy at best. The European landscape is littered with isolated but not strategically significant monuments to defence cooperation. The UK, Germany, Italy and Spain have previously cooperated on the Eurofighter Typhoon aircraft. There is a European Air Transport Command, which involves seven member states of the EU in sharing access to strategic lift capabilities. Some bilateral initiatives clearly are worthwhile and notable too: the Belgian and Dutch navies have been deeply integrated since 1996. The UK and France signed the Lancaster House Treaties of 2010, in which the two countries agreed to deeper nuclear cooperation, to some sharing of equipment and capabilities, and to the setting up of a Combined Joint Expeditionary Force, among other things.

In late 2017, the EU also had seventeen Common Security and Defence Policy (CSDP) missions deployed in the field. These are military or civilian–military missions that cover activities as far apart as counter-piracy operations off the coast of Somalia, efforts to identify, capture and dispose of vessels engaged in migrant trafficking in the Mediterranean, and providing support, advice and training to police, gendarmerie and national guard forces in Mali. Other missions are deployed in Kosovo, Ukraine, Georgia and Afghanistan, to name just a few. These are all worthwhile developments and deployments. What none of them represents, however, is the projection of serious military power by a European Union on the verge of standing on its own two feet when it comes to defence.

A status quo of nationally led approaches to defence planning and procurement still persists, resulting in serious European defence capability gaps. One study suggests that at a cost of almost half of US defence expenditure, the EU28 obtains only a tenth of the deployable capability. This in turn means the EU lacks any strategic autonomy and is heavily dependent on the US. When the EU talks of renewed defence ambition, it is also perhaps worth remembering that efforts to move towards common European defence have been an integral part of the European project since at least 1950, the year in which French Prime Minister René Pleven proposed the setting up of a European army and the appointment of a European minister of defence. Pleven's proposal ultimately turned into the Treaty Establishing the European Defence Community, and was signed by the six founding members of the European Coal and Steel Community on 27 May 1952. This astonishing treaty, signed only seven years after the conclusion of World War Two, was subsequently ratified by Germany and the Benelux countries. It envisaged a common European army with forty divisions of 13,000 soldiers each, all serving in a common uniform and being paid for out of a common defence budget, underpinned by joint military procurement and common institutions. Ultimately, it never came into force because the French themselves baulked at ratification. More than six decades later, the idea of a common European army is no nearer coming to fruition and has no serious support on the continent. What is even more telling than the failure to deliver on this exalted ambition, however, is that progress has not even extended to serious national capabilities being effectively combined on large-scale operations, absent the presence and support of the United States.

Of related concern, there is little evidence that EU sanctions have fundamentally changed Russian behaviour. President Putin has carried on regardless, and far from being cowed, his behaviour in relation to Ukraine, North Korea and Syria has demonstrated a willingness to throw Russian diplomatic and military weight about not only in Russia's own neighbourhood but in places well beyond it. Whereas the hope was that EU sanctions, which were also backed by the United States and others, would hurt some of Russia's new rich and persuade them to withdraw support for Putin's policies, the reality inside Russia has been far different. Putin's brutal treatment of disloyal oligarchs such as Mikhail Khodorkovsky and Boris Berezovsky, and his track record of rewarding those who are loyal, has, up to now, kept his internal position secure.

In fact, there are relatively few examples of international sanctions achieving their primary diplomatic objective of changing an adversary's policies. Iran offers a good recent example of success but the list of failures in this area of policy is long. The real goal in using them is often to show symbolic displeasure with an actor on the international stage or to answer the domestic call that, in the face of an international crisis or outrage, something must be done. In a world so globalised and interdependent, it is also difficult to construct sanctions policies that do not damage one's own domestic economic interests. All of this complexity been evident in the EU's sanctions policy on Russia. The sanctions themselves are a public response to Russian behaviour. But while they have been targeted at important Russian individuals and sectors they have also been restrained for domestic reasons. More serious financial sanctions would have damaged a number of interests in the City of London. French resolve has been checked by the political and economic stakes involved in defence contracts signed with Russia. German auto and energy interests have also acted as voices urging restraint. Some central and eastern European EU member states that are heavily dependent on Russian energy supplies have also been reluctant to go in too hard. Even in Latvia, with more to fear from Russian aggression than most, one hears calls for restraint, reflecting the extent to which its economy is tied to that of Russia. It is not, in the end therefore, possible to disentangle this complex reality from the failure of the sanctions regime to have greater effect.

It is perhaps only on the challenge of migration where the measures taken in response to the EU's current crisis have achieved a significant impact. Here, the steps taken have resulted in a major reduction in the numbers of refugees and migrants arriving in the EU. The European Union Border and Coastguard Agency has been running major operations to interdict people smugglers and to rescue vessels and individuals in distress in the Mediterranean, especially in the waters close to Greece and Italy. There has been a policy of paying others, outside the EU, to stop the flows of people arriving in Europe and to dissuade them from even making it to the Mediterranean. One element of this approach has been pursued at an EU-wide level. On 18 March 2016, the EU signed a deal with Turkey in which the Turkish authorities agreed both to take back large numbers of irregular migrants who had arrived in the EU via Turkey, and to act to stop any future flows. In return, the EU agreed to provide €3 billion to Turkey to help cover the costs of refugees living there, with a possible further €3 billion to be made available by the end of 2018. In addition, the EU committed to accelerate its consideration of a visa liberalisation agreement with Turkey so the latter's citizens might soon be able to travel to the EU without the need for a visa. The EU also agreed to re-energise talks on Turkey's possible entry into the EU at some point in future and to engage in renewed efforts to upgrade Turkey's relationship with the EU's customs union.[65]

Another strand of policy has come from individual EU member states, principally Italy and France. Faced with continued large-scale flows of people arriving via Libya, the

Italian authorities decided in 2017 to take matters into their own hands. The country's interior minister, Marco Minniti, engaged directly with Libyan tribal leaders and mayors of towns afflicted with people trafficking. In what he calls 'a type of pact' Minniti has promised that Italy will help to replace the bad-money economy that has arisen out of trafficking in these places with a good-money economy based on other types of economic activity. His offer to local leaders is essentially: 'You help us to stop the human traffickers and we will free you from their blackmail.'[66] Another feature of the former spymaster's approach has been to stop some NGO aid ships from rescuing migrants when their boats capsize in the Mediterranean, the implication being that the existence of those ships encourages the flow of migrants and leads to NGOs effectively operating in cahoots with people smugglers. This latter set of measures has been hugely controversial, not least because many who study the underlying causes and motivations of irregular migration don't believe it can be stopped simply by making the journey riskier. Desperate people, often fleeing conflict zones, are driven to do desperate things.

Nonetheless, so impressed with the Italians' progress was France's newly elected President, Emmanuel Macron, that in August 2017 he hosted a mini-summit of leaders from France, Italy, Spain, Germany, Chad, Niger and one of the factions in Libya, declaring that 'what has been done by Italy and Libya is a perfect example of what we are aiming for'. The meeting, held in Paris, proposed measures for EU aid programmes for the transit countries, in an attempt to give people more of an economic reason to stay in Africa and less of a reason to attempt the journey to Europe. It also discussed the setting up of migrant reception centres in Chad and Niger to allow preliminary assessment of asylum applications there, and the provision of special border security support for both these countries. While the EU has talked publicly about welcoming some migrants, of distributing them across the continent, and of their effective integration into European society therefore, the policy it has pursued in practice has been one of interdiction oiled by cash.

The EU collectively, and Italy in particular, has received heavy criticism for its pursuit of this approach. Some have rightly argued that the policy has been callously enacted with little regard for the EU's legal obligations to migrants and refugees. Justified though that criticism may be, it is important to also understand that the EU settled on this policy haphazardly, not as its first preference but as a consequence of its inability to agree on doing anything else.

At the peak of the migration crisis in September 2015, the German Chancellor, Angela Merkel, effectively threw open the doors to Germany and declared refugees and migrants welcome. It is said that she did not consult other EU leaders before making her decision. Such is her authority, however, that her position set in train an effort to take a pan-European and pro-humanitarian approach to the crisis. At its heart, this involved the proposal that each member state should agree to take a fair share of those arriving in Europe in search of a better life. Merkel's stance was initially greeted by many as the hallmark of humane and progressive European leadership. Many Germans rallied round to provide offers of assistance to their country's new arrivals, and Merkel herself declared her confidence that Germany was both ready and able to rise to the challenge. It did not take long, however, before she was met with a brutal political backlash in her own country and with exasperation and resistance in other parts of Europe.

In Germany, that backlash ultimately propelled the highly anti-immigrant and nationalist Alternative für Deutschland into the Bundestag with ninety-two seats in the general election of 2017. While Merkel was re-elected as Chancellor, her party, the CDU, suffered its worst results for almost seven decades and she was left struggling to piece together a functioning coalition. Outside Germany the Austrian leadership, faced with large flows of migrants passing through Austria from the Balkans en route to southern Germany, reimposed border checks that had been removed as part of the Schengen Agreement. They also set paltry daily limits on numbers of applications for asylum and transit that they were willing to process. Hungary took a very hard line, using water cannon and tear gas on crowds of migrants at the border with Serbia, and putting up a razor wire border fence on both the Serbian and Croatian borders to keep the refugees and migrants out. The authorities in Budapest made clear they would prosecute any migrants found to have entered the country illegally. Prime Minister Viktor Orbán couldn't have been clearer about who he considered responsible for what was going on, openly blaming the German leadership for encouraging the influx by welcoming so many migrants. His tough position was largely supported by other central European countries including Slovakia, Poland and the Czech Republic. These four countries, known as the Visegrád 4 or V4 group, have vociferously opposed the EU quota plan for distributing migrants across Europe ever since.

Other divisions were also opened up between member states. The Austrians accused Greece, the country that saw almost 900,000 refugees and economic migrants arrive by sea in 2015, of simply waving migrants through to the rest of Europe without any attempt to control the flow. Greece, for its part, already crippled economically, insisted that it did not have the resources to be Europe's holding centre for refugees. Italy, a country also on the front line, receiving large numbers of migrants across the Mediterranean from Libya, frequently and persistently expressed its anger that other EU countries were unwilling to take on a fair share of the burden while its own reception centres were overcrowded.

Further north, the French authorities reintroduced border controls at the Belgian border, in light of evidence that the terrorists responsible for the November 2015 attack in Paris had entered the country from Belgium, after using the western Balkan migrant route to re-enter Europe from Syria. The build-up of migrants living rough near Calais also caused tension between the UK and France. As thousands awaited an opportunity to travel legally or illegally to the United Kingdom, the French authorities eventually forcibly removed migrants and demolished the makeshift 'jungle' refugee camp there. Even in Scandinavia, despite an enormously welcoming response initially from Sweden, which received 160,000 migrants in 2015, the highest number per capita of any country in Europe, the response soon became more hard-line. Sweden reintroduced border identity checks for people travelling from Denmark in an attempt to limit migrant numbers, a move that caused considerable delays to daily traffic at the border. Denmark itself took one of the toughest positions in the whole of Europe, giving the police the authority to seize valuables worth more than £1,000 from migrants to help pay for the cost of their food and accommodation.

These divisions and tensions within the EU were laid bare in a European Court of Justice (ECJ) case in September 2017. Hungary and Slovakia mounted a legal case against the quota system that had been agreed by a majority of EU states at a European Council meeting at the height of the crisis in 2015. Supported by other east European states, including a relatively new right-wing Polish government that had reversed the support for quotas offered by its predecessor, the Hungarians and Slovaks sought to contest moves to relocate 120,000 migrants from Syria and elsewhere across the EU. They were opposed in court by the European Commission, Greece, Italy, Germany, Sweden and several other member states. The ECJ dismissed the Slovakian and Hungarian case, arguing that even those states who had opposed the policy were bound under EU law to implement it.

After the ruling was made public, Péter Szijjártó, the Hungarian foreign minister, said his government considered the decision to be 'appalling and irresponsible'. Beata Szydło, the Polish Prime Minister, said Poland had expected the ruling but that it would 'not change the position of the Polish government on migration policy'. In response, the EU Migration Commissioner, Greece's Dimitris Avramopoulos, said the quota system was mandatory, that EU states should show solidarity on the issue 'because it is clear some member states need solidarity' and that any country refusing to comply would face further ECJ action and the possible levying of daily fines for non-compliance.[67] Despite his tough stance, by September 2017 only 25,000 of the 120,000 migrants in line for relocation had been moved.

Behind the rhetoric surrounding calls for deeper

European integration, and across the ongoing effort to find common responses to other dimensions of the EU's crisis, this lack of solidarity and presence of division forms the constant leitmotif. While the formal display of EU unity on the Russia sanctions has been impressive, for example, the reality is that behind the scenes, deep divisions exist among EU member states. The Poles and the three Baltic states have generally been more hawkish. Hungary, Slovakia and Bulgaria are more 'understanding' of Russia's position. In western Europe, Britain has tended to side with the east European hawks more often than not, which is precisely why some in eastern Europe are now worried that a knock-on effect of Brexit will be a weakening of the EU sanctions regime on Russia. The Germans are traditionally in favour of maintaining dialogue with Russia. Italy, Spain, Greece and Greek Cyprus are opposed to punishing Russia and prefer to engage with it through diplomacy. The upshot has been an EU response to Russian behaviour that has achieved the secondary objective of showing displeasure and a willingness to act while failing entirely in its primary purpose. No one could reasonably claim the sanctions have changed Russian behaviour. The fact that the sanctions are reviewed and extended at six-month intervals is also telling. Since the sanctions are linked to implementation of the Minsk Agreement, it would be possible to extend them until implementation is evident. In practice, the regular reviews and extensions are the price paid by those most in favour of the sanctions to keep the countries least in favour of them on board.

On defence cooperation, some of the divisions inside the EU are strategic. The EU's efforts to cooperate with NATO notwithstanding, one major source of disagreement concerns the extent to which the EU really should strive for autonomy in defence. A number of countries believe that no autonomous European defence capability could be built without undermining NATO. This has traditionally been a concern for the UK but it goes much wider and explains why Donald Trump's presidency is such a potential trauma for east Europeans in particular. In Warsaw, Tallinn, Vilnius and Riga, a security guarantee from Brussels carries nothing like the same weight as one from Washington. The French on the other hand have traditionally had a reluctance to rely excessively on the US, the lead player in NATO, and are often the ones, rhetorically at least, pushing the EU defence dimension hardest.

Other divisions on this issue are a function of geography. The countries in the east of Europe fear Russia the most and believe deterring it should be the primary focus for Europe's defence. Several countries in the south on the other hand are focused more on the increasingly severe challenges emanating from the Middle East and Africa. In addition, national histories and strategic cultures differ greatly among EU member states. Among those that in principle support stronger European defence and security cooperation, such as Germany, France, the Benelux countries, Italy and Spain, some of these differences are manifest in debates over when and where it is appropriate to use military force. France has a strong tradition of willingness to use its forces on expeditionary operations and decisions on this are taken by a strong executive branch of government. Germany, for historical reasons, has strong Bundestag oversight of any military activity and a much greater reluctance to deploy forces elsewhere in Europe or in high-risk environments outside it. A number of EU countries, such as Ireland, Austria and Finland, have positions of 'neutrality'. This all puts a question mark over the ability of Europeans to agree on what needs to be done in response to any particular security threat, and without such agreement, there is an understandable reluctance to rely too much on the EU for defence. Jean-Claude Juncker can deliver as many speeches calling for a Defence Union as he likes, but none of them will supplant the limiting effects of these deep historical, political, geographic and strategic divergences and complexities.

Despite the disastrous implications of current defence industrial approaches, EU member states are also still reluctant to look beyond national industrial champions when considering procurement. This reluctance is based on a desire to maintain capabilities that are considered of national strategic, not only economic, importance; on the need to ensure security of supply of essential defence capabilities and the skills capable of delivering them; and on the desire to protect local jobs and supply chains. This is all perfectly understandable. But boil it all down and what it means is that progress is stymied by a mixture of local pork barrel politics and a lack of mutual trust among EU members. As a consequence, the EU will remain incapable of standing on its own two feet on defence and security for many, many years to come. It will remain highly vulnerable to destabilisation from outside forces against which it has little effective protection.

More fundamental still for the European project as a whole are the deep divisions that exist among EU members on the future management of the eurozone. Some of the remaining weaknesses in the political and institutional architecture of the single currency have been highlighted in this chapter. Those weaknesses reflect disagreements over how best to put the single currency's future beyond doubt. The division between France and Germany, or to be more precise, between the German tradition of ordo-liberal economics and the French commitment to Keynesianism, is central.[68] Both of these traditions of economic thinking believe that unfettered markets are inherently unstable. But while the latter sees a role for the state in using public spending to boost demand during economic downturns, an approach the eurozone badly lacked in the recent crisis and has still not fully embraced, the former focuses its attention almost entirely on state intervention to set the rules within which markets can operate effectively. Ordo-liberals have virtually nothing to say about how to handle depressions or the problem of the German trade surplus, two issues that are absolutely crucial to the future stability of the eurozone.

Nonetheless, ordo-liberal thinking is dominant in Germany and Germany is dominant in the eurozone. Deep scepticism exists in Germany towards French ideas on how the eurozone might be reformed because those ideas are seen as an ill-disguised attempt to access German money while loosening German control.[69] More explicitly, French reform ideas are seen as cover for an attempt to practice Keynesian-style demand management not at national but at eurozone level. Chancellor Merkel has been careful not to reject President Macron's ideas for a fiscal union out of hand, but they will most likely be gutted of real substance because of this suspicion, meaning that any further reform that does come will almost certainly be superficial. Macron, far from loosening the fiscal stance in France, is therefore actually cutting government spending in an attempt to demonstrate a renewed French commitment to fiscal rectitude to a sceptical German audience.

The grounds for scepticism about overcoming these differences are not just practical but historical. Macron's eurozone reform proposals are not dissimilar to those of both

Nicolas Sarkozy and François Hollande before him. And as Yanis Varoufakis, the former finance minister of Greece, has pointed out, the Franco-German divide on the single currency can in fact be traced back as far as the 1960s.[70] This dance is a long one, and so far it has always ended pretty much where it began, with little progress towards genuine integration of eurozone economic policy.

While France and Germany clearly see a need to reinforce the eurozone, they are therefore extremely unlikely to agree on how to do it. Other important divisions on this issue, beyond those between the French and Germans, also exist. Some of these are between the nineteen EU member states that are members of the eurozone and the nine that are not. The nine outside the euro are rightly suspicious of any attempt to pursue a multi-speed Europe that leaves them locked into an outer fringe of the European Union and with their interests subordinated to French and German designs. If the eurozone core does genuinely seek a path to deeper integration, this could easily provoke resistance and a much wider divide between those EU states that have the euro as their currency and those that do not.[71] The questions over the future stability of the single currency remain, therefore, not only because of the gaps and remaining weaknesses in the euro's institutional architecture, but because of serious doubts as to whether EU member states will be able to agree to do anything effective about them.

If one stands back to take stock of how the EU has responded to the many crises facing it today, one is left with two emotions. The first is some appreciation of the activity and effort expended in trying to drive the European project forward. This has not been inconsiderable and it should be respected. The second is that it is just not enough to mask deep underlying divisions. The truth is that the governments of the EU remain divided over how to respond. There are deep, possibly unbridgeable, disagreements over how best to handle the flows of migrants heading to Europe from the Middle East, sub-Saharan Africa and central Asia; equally deep disagreements over how to handle Putin's Russia; and divisions over how to strengthen monetary union. Member states of the EU, and coalitions of member states, are lining up and locking horns with each other across this range of issues. The debate itself has become toxic and damaging, with economic disagreements feeding anti-German sentiment in southern Europe on the one hand and accusations of Mediterranean laxity becoming commonplace in political debate in several northern member states on the other. East European states are deeply suspicious that their allies in the south and west are actively looking for ways to reduce the sanctions pressure on Russia and to sell them out. Meanwhile many in the south of Europe believe east European members have a blind spot when it comes to dealing not only with Russia but with the challenge of migration. Almost everywhere, the dominance of short-term, tactical and national political calculation over long-term strategic thought and European solidarity appears prevalent. While a degree of disagreement and debate is inevitable among such a large group of states, the inescapable conclusion, for me at least, is that the EU remains fragile and vulnerable to a sudden worsening of economic and political conditions. Such is its fragility, in fact, that one or more trigger events could now precipitate its collapse.

PART 2

COLLAPSE
AND ITS
CONSEQUENCES

CHAPTER 6

TRIGGERS OF DISINTEGRATION

The plausibility of trigger events and EU collapse scenarios is obviously in the eye of the beholder. In this chapter, I identify six such triggers that I consider to be plausible enough. I have divided them into two broad categories. The first category centres on the possibility of a renewed economic crisis and what could be its political consequences. In this category, I examine two trigger events, the first being a new recession and the second a new financial crisis. The second category involves events that are not primarily economic but political and security related. Here I identify four plausible triggers: a Eurosceptic populist breakthrough in the eurozone core; the spiralling effects of a secession crisis in a European Union member state; the possible breakdown of the EU–Turkey deal on migration; and an attempt to create a deeper and more extensive fiscal union that ultimately provokes a severe political backlash. Each of these is outlined in turn.

CATEGORY 1:
A RENEWED ECONOMIC CRISIS

Trigger 1: A renewed recession

As noted in the introduction to this book, there are many inside the EU currently breathing a sigh of relief that the worst is over with regard to the economic crisis. Current projected growth rates for the eurozone of around 2 per cent a year are a big improvement over what much of the continent experienced between 2008 and 2016, and unemployment rates are falling. The danger of a renewed recession however, is real.

Perhaps the biggest external threat to eurozone growth comes from Donald Trump. Both Trump's management of the US economy and his approach to international trade have the potential to trigger a slow-down in Europe. Inside the US, if growth disappoints and the Trump administration slides further into chaos, the effect could be a loss of confidence in the US dollar and a concomitant increase in the value of the euro. This would hit eurozone exports and growth. Internationally, if Trump's more aggressive stance on trade were to provoke a bout of global protectionism, this too could be deeply damaging. In 2017, the eurozone was running a trade surplus with the rest of the world to the tune of about 3.5 per cent of GDP, a sizeable chunk of it with the US. This, and the German–US trade surplus in particular, has been the subject of several Trump outbursts.

If the President were to continue to undermine the World Trade Organization by stealth to the point where it ceased functioning, or if he were to turn his harsh trade rhetoric into action, there is no doubt that the disruption to euro-zone economies would be substantial.

Elsewhere on the international scene, there are concerns about the possible effects of a financial crisis in China. While China is still not as pivotal as the US to the international financial system, it is becoming so. It is also experiencing a rapid growth of both public and private debt. If this is not effectively managed and ends in a crash, the slow-down in Chinese growth would hurt the whole global economy, including the eurozone. Closer to home, were the UK to crash out of the EU without a Brexit deal, or were a conflict in the Middle East to result in a sudden increase in the oil price and an interruption in supply, these events too would cause negative impacts on the eurozone's prospects. Developments inside Europe could also contribute to the risks. One big question mark concerns how long the ECB will be able to maintain its current approach to monetary policy. The longer the recovery goes on, the more pressure Mario Draghi will be under to tighten it. If the ECB gets this wrong by raising interest rates or tapering its quantita-tive easing programme too aggressively, its decisions could damage growth and help tip the eurozone back into reces-sion.[72] It is also possible that a combination of some of the developments speculated on above could come together in something like a perfect storm.

If the potential causes of recession are there, why might this trigger an EU collapse? The most obvious path from recession to EU collapse, it seems to me, passes through a new sovereign debt and banking crisis. In a really deep recession, the public finances of eurozone member states would take a hammering. Countries with already high debt-to-GDP ratios before the new recession began would be likely to see their borrowing costs rise sharply and the value of their own sovereign bonds fall steeply. This would in turn damage the balance sheets of their banks. Asset values would decline, non-performing loans would increase and banks still weighed down by the legacy of non-performing loans left by the last crisis would be in trouble, not least because many of them are heavily invested in their own government's bonds. Given that the provisions in the Banking Union are not operating consistently, and that the Single Resolution Fund is not backed by sufficient resource, a convincing collective European response would be unlikely. Confidence in the banks would quickly come to depend on confidence in the sovereigns that stood behind them. It is therefore probable that before long, and as discussed in the last chapter, the state–bank doom loop would once again come into operation. Governments with already high debt-to-GDP ratios, worsening fiscal outlooks and demands that they bail out failing banks afresh would find it difficult to persuade markets that they could avoid defaults.

In that scenario, one way for the eurozone to respond would be to restructure a sufficient portion of the existing sovereign debt of the countries in trouble. A partial restructuring was eventually accepted for Greece but for the most part, even there, it has been resisted. Greece still labours under the burden of a massive debt. Restructuring is therefore extremely unlikely on a larger scale.

This would leave dealing with the renewed crisis through use of the European Stability Mechanism (ESM). Here, however, the key question would be which countries were at the forefront of the crisis and whether the ESM was big enough to handle it. But even assuming that it was, a very dubious assumption if we were dealing with economies the size of Spain or Italy, its use would trigger two political dynamics. The first would be the interstate dynamic that pits countries needing to stand behind the ESM against those needing to access funds through it. This is deeply divisive and undermining to any effort to build a sense of European solidarity. The second would be the austerity dynamic within the countries in trouble. As already noted, ESM help comes with conditions. Depending on the specific country and circumstances, these conditions might mean spending cuts and changes to the tax system, labour laws, pensions and social programmes. Whatever the mix, countries in trouble would be staring down the barrel of a gun. If they wanted to stay in the eurozone, there would be more austerity at home and the toxification of relations between them and their wealthier EU creditors abroad.

It is my contention that, after what much of Europe has been through in the last decade, there is no guarantee that such a response could command public and political support. Deals might be struck in the short term to implement such measures and everyone might breathe a sigh of relief. But what ought to have been learned from the last crisis is that politics sometimes takes time to catch up with the effects of economic policy choices. The political dynamics unleashed could unfold quickly, or over time. They would likely include the destabilisation of governments introducing austerity, early elections to test support for reforms, and a significant boost to Eurosceptic populist parties who would reject the austerity medicine and argue in favour of leaving the euro or the EU altogether. At the point at which one significant country was in such a predicament and its exit from the euro was possible, moreover, contagion to others would most likely follow. A scenario in which multiple countries are forced to the brink of exit is therefore feasible in a severe recession. Nothing in the raft of measures introduced to strengthen the euro so far has taken this scenario off the table. And while some might argue that technically, the unravelling of the euro does not have to mean the collapse of the EU, in practice it is likely to mean exactly that, a case I make more fully in the next chapter.

Trigger 2: An Italian banking crisis

If a recession does not trigger a banking crisis there is a non-negligible possibility that a new banking crisis could be the trigger for a deep recession. The context that makes this a concern has both a global and a specifically European dimension and the two, of course, are linked. Warnings of another global financial crisis are coming fairly thick and fast. In September 2017, former UK Prime Minister Gordon Brown warned of the risks to the global financial system that could come from the scale of unregulated 'shadow banking' in Asia.[73] A week later, Wolfgang Schäuble made a similar warning, but pointed to the scale of asset bubbles created by the trillions of dollars pumped into world markets by central bank quantitative easing programmes as a major source of concern. Bubbles, he warned, could turn into a crash and eventual withdrawal of quantitative easing measures or increases in interest rates could be the triggers.[74] Schäuble's remarks chimed with those of Christine Lagarde, the head of the International Monetary Fund, who warned not only about debt levels but of a return to 'excessive risk taking' in financial markets. For 'excessive risk taking' read irresponsible, unregulated lending using often complex and difficult to understand instruments that make it unclear who really owes what to whom.

At European level, the banking system has still not recovered from the last crisis. Significant pockets of bad debt persist. In both Italy and Spain there have been recent bank failures and a mix of bail-in (Spain) and bail-out (Italy) instruments was required to deal with them. The threat of bail-ins under the new European Single Resolution Mechanism (SRM) has increased the cost of borrowing to some weak banks and weakened them still further.[75] Italy is a particular black-spot and there is much speculation that it could become the epicentre of a new euro crisis. Danske Bank reported in August 2017 that just over 17 per cent of all Italian bank loans were non-performing, amounting to a total of €349 billion.[76] If the banks in a country like Italy suffered major unexpected losses as a result of an external shock that depreciated the value of assets on their balance sheets or deepened and expanded their problem with non-performing loans, they would quickly be in trouble.

If this happens, two possible paths will be open to the Italian authorities. They could follow the new rules of the SRM, including bailing in holders of Italian bank bonds, or they could instead use Italian taxpayers' money to bail out the banks. The attraction of taking the first option is that it would limit the extent to which Italian taxpayers had to support the banks and would therefore be less likely to trigger market concerns about the ability of the Italian state to pay its own debts. Attractive though that thought may be, however, it is unlikely that the Italian authorities would choose this course of action. The reason for this is that ordinary Italian savers and families are large-scale holders of Italian bank bonds and would be massive losers in the event of such a bail-in. This is why, in the case of the Banco Monte dei Paschi di Siena, the authorities opted to use taxpayers' money to bail out the failing bank rather than to adopt Banking Union bail-in procedures. When a bail-in was used to resolve four smaller banks in 2015, moreover, protests and suicides followed.[77] Such an approach would likely cause a run on the banks anyway and capital flight to other jurisdictions. The ensuing chaos would not only tail-spin the economy but further damage the balance sheets of the banks. Attempting bail-ins as a response to a systemic banking crisis in Italy could also have profound political consequences. The country has already suffered two lost decades of economic growth and faces a significant Eurosceptic populist uprising. The application of what would be seen as European bail-in rules to such a crisis, while damaging Italian savers in the process, could give Eurosceptic populist parties their biggest boost in years and trigger a political path to euro exit.

This, perhaps, is one reason why there has been persistent conflict between national banking regulators and politicians in Italy and the European Single Resolution Board, the permanent body set up to monitor and deal with Europe's struggling banks. Even if Italy did try to go down this route it would run into the problem of insufficient funds available to the Single Resolution Fund (SRF). It has never really been anticipated that in the event of a systemic crisis, the SRF would be the sole required response. But even those more optimistic about the fund acknowledge that if a crisis occurs while the fund is being built up between now and 2024, it will almost certainly be inadequate.[78] By September 2017, via levies on the banks, it had reached only €17 billion. Given that the SRF would not be enough, the question of who or what ultimately stands behind it if it runs out of money would arise. The difficulty in agreeing the details of a common European backstop for the fund was noted in the last chapter. Taxpayers elsewhere in Europe, and their political leaders, would not want to stump up additional support to help resolve and recapitalise Italian or other banks they consider to have been badly, irresponsibly or in some cases corruptly managed. This is the reason why agreeing the common backstop to the SRF has been so difficult in the first place.

Given the serious political unpalatability and likely unworkability of the 'European' bail-in option, the preferred choice of the Italian leadership, trapped between a rock and a hard place, might be to try to handle the crisis by using bail-outs. Indeed, whether via a tried and failed attempt to handle the crisis with European Banking Union rules, or via an Italian decision not to go down the EBU route in the first place, it would quickly become clear that the real backstop behind struggling Italian banks was the Italian government itself. The problem with this is that Italy already has a very large debt-to-GDP ratio of over 130 per cent. Adding more debt could trigger fresh concern about Italy's ability to service those debts, especially given its prolonged anaemic rates of economic growth.

In that eventuality, the dynamic that would unfold is not dissimilar to the one outlined in the first trigger event above. The eurozone has not been able to agree on the full restructuring of Greece's much smaller sovereign debt so an agreed restructuring of Italy's massive public debt would be politically out of the question and would not therefore provide a way out. The Italian authorities could try to turn to the ESM to keep the state solvent but if they did so, they would face politically very unpopular conditions. After many years of little or no growth, it is just as likely that Italian voters would increase their support for populist parties promising another path. To avoid this outcome, even a mainstream Italian government, faced with the choice of austerity inside the euro or the uncertain path of life outside it, might choose the latter as the only way to stay relevant in what would be a new political climate. Whether via the bail-in route or the bail-out route, there is a plausible path to a euro exit buried in the Italian banking crisis.

CATEGORY 2: POLITICAL CRISES

Trigger 3: A Eurosceptic breakthrough
in a large EU member state

One of the more obvious possible routes to EU break-up is through a Eurosceptic electoral victory in one of the EU's larger core member states. The two most likely culprits here, now the UK has opted for Brexit, are France and Italy. The relief with which Emmanuel Macron's second-round defeat of Marine Le Pen in the May 2017 French presidential election was met was palpable across Europe. It was a convincing victory, 66 per cent to Le Pen's 34 per cent. Macron's new party, La République En Marche!, also won a majority in the parliamentary elections that followed a month or so later. There is, however, another analysis of the French election cycle that is far more worrying. In the first round of the presidential election, Macron polled just over 8.6 million votes to Marine Le Pen's 7.7 million. From the far left, Jean-Luc Mélenchon polled 7 million. Sandwiched between Le Pen and Mélenchon was François Fillon from the centre-right Républicains with 7.2 million votes. The vote was therefore quite evenly split among the four leading candidates and it is worth taking a look at what the candidates opposing Macron chose to run on. From an EU perspective, it does not make for happy reading.

Le Pen got much of the media attention and given that for much of the campaign she was polling second and ultimately made it to the second-round run-off, that is understandable. Though for much of the recent past unambiguously in favour of a French exit from the EU and the euro, she modified her stance in 2017 to say she would try to renegotiate France's entire relationship with the EU over a six-month period if she became President. At the end of that period, if her attempt failed, she would put the issue of euro membership to the country in a referendum. Importantly for many of the Eurosceptic movements across Europe that claim they would like to lead their own countries down a similar path, Le Pen claimed that the process of a euro exit would not be chaotic nor lead to economic catastrophe. She denied that exiting the euro would lead to a run on French banks and stressed she wanted to achieve French exit without 'breaking the dishes', suggesting it would be possible to do so in consultation with other European countries. She also argued that a string of other countries 'suffering' euro membership, such as Italy, Spain and Greece, would follow France out of the single currency, and talked vaguely of returning to a process of managed exchange rate flexibility in Europe, of the kind experienced under the Exchange Rate Mechanism and European Currency Unit system that preceded the euro.[79]

Her dubious claims about the possibility of a non-chaotic exit from the single currency will be returned to in the next chapter. For now, it is enough to note her position and to note that not only on the single currency but on much else besides, her views were and are incompatible with many aspects of EU membership. She campaigned for protectionism rather than for the single market, suggesting she would impose an import tax of 3 per cent. She threatened to ignore EU competition rules, so that public bodies in France could use their procurement programmes to buy French as much as possible. And she made clear that, if elected, she would suspend France's membership of the Schengen border-free zone and end free movement.

Jean-Luc Mélenchon's position was not wholly dissimilar. The 65-year-old disgruntled former member of the Socialist Party emerged as the star of the anti-Macron campaign, putting up very strong TV debate and interview performances and surging in support during the campaign itself. He tapped into deep-seated economic discontent with a proposal to tax 100 per cent of any person's revenue that was twenty times greater than the median income. He said he wanted France to quit NATO and pursue warmer ties with President Putin while working with Syria's President Bashar al-Assad in the fight against ISIS. And on the EU, like Le Pen, he argued for the complete renegotiation of France's relationship with it, stating that, if the negotiation didn't bring the hoped-for results, it would be up to the French people to decide in a referendum whether to remain in the bloc.[80] By 'renegotiate', what Mélenchon meant was an exit from existing European treaties, 'by abandoning the existing rules for all the countries that wish it and the negotiation of other rules'.[81] More specifically, he wanted an end to the independence of the European Central Bank, without which he would be in favour of a French exit from the euro. He called for a conference to agree the rescheduling and partial cancellation of European sovereign debt. And he demanded a more protectionist policy between the EU and the rest of the world. To strengthen his hand in negotiations were he to become President, he threatened to stop French contributions to the EU budget and to put in place controls on the movement of capital and goods at France's borders. Some have also noted an important anti-German sentiment in Mélenchon's thinking, quoting him as saying: 'Germany is again a danger. Its imperialism is returning and the EU is its new empire.'[82]

One can argue about the wisdom and workability of some of Mélenchon's proposals, and more debate about some of them would be a good thing, because as noted earlier, the EU and especially the eurozone have allowed themselves at times to become trapped in damaging economic dogma. One cannot argue, however, that Mélenchon wanted anything other than the destruction of the EU as currently constituted. Working with other far-left leaders across Europe, his threat was, in effect, to destroy the EU as is and build a new, more left-wing one in its place. On the details of transition between one and the other, there was largely silence.

What ought to set alarm bells ringing just as much as the position of these two Eurosceptic contenders for the Elysée, however, was the position taken up in the campaign by François Fillon, the candidate for the so-called mainstream centre-right Républicains. Fillon declared he was in favour of France staying in the EU but he called for reforms to it and in tone, he can hardly be accused of running a pro-EU campaign. He accused the 'Brussels machine of running on empty, or worse, eroding freedoms, with mixed results at best'.[83] He said France should ignore the Schengen open-borders regime because France's partners in the EU could not be trusted to protect their borders properly.[84] And he implied that Muslim immigration was a threat to French identity. 'Catholics, Protestants and Jews don't denounce the values of the republic,' he is reported to have said, leading some to accuse him of aping Marine Le Pen in an attempt to boost his poll ratings.[85]

Between them, Fillon, Le Pen and Mélenchon polled 22 million votes to Macron's 8.6 million in the first round. This represents a 60 per cent vote for candidates who were either openly in favour of France leaving the EU or the euro, if they could not be fundamentally reformed, or for a candidate who thought it a good idea to kick the EU hard in order to get traction with the public. The fact that most ultimately chose the pro-EU Macron when the only other choice in the second round was Le Pen is more a reflection of the constrained second-round choice offered to voters by French election procedure than it is a demonstration of national sentiment. In the parliamentary elections, moreover, although Macron's La République En Marche! and its centrist allies in the Mouvement Démocrate won a large majority of seats, in both the first and the second round of voting turnout was less than 50 per cent. It is therefore hard to see the 2017 French election cycle as a ringing endorsement of the EU. France is a country whose politics are both volatile and febrile. If Macron fails in his attempts to fundamentally improve the lives of many French citizens, the indications are there that an extreme and very Eurosceptic candidate will be in with a strong chance of winning the presidency in 2022.

The situation in Italy is hardly more reassuring. Recent changes to the Italian constitution mean two thirds of parliamentary seats will be decided by proportional representation and the other third by first-past-the-post votes in constituencies.[86] These measures may work against the likelihood of a populist breakthrough. However, if the opinion polls are anywhere near accurate, there is little room for complacency. For much of 2017 the populist and very Eurosceptic Five Star Movement was polling neck and neck with or just ahead of the centre-left Democratic Party, making it just about the most popular political party in the country. Another Eurosceptic party, the Northern League, was polling in third place. Between them, the two parties had something in the region of 43 per cent support. As in France, these levels of support may ultimately prove very significant as harbingers of a mood taking hold in the country. Discontent with the status quo is rife. The only question is who or what will be the political beneficiary.

Arguably, Five Star ought to be dead and buried in political terms given that in the recent past it has suffered serious internal divisions. Its perceived mismanagement of matters in Rome since its candidate there, Virginia Raggi, was elected mayor in 2016, also ought to have damaged its credibility. But it remains a serious contender for power. Its recently elected leader and candidate for Prime Minister, the 31-year-old Luigi Di Maio, echoes both Le Pen and Mélenchon when he says his party wants to stay in the EU but 'change a number of treaties that are hurting our economy and our businesses'.[87] The party also wants to call a consultative referendum on Italy's membership of the euro. One of the movement's most charismatic leading figures and a possible future foreign minister, Alessandro Di Battista, has also said publicly that he would oppose euro membership in any referendum because 'a country that cannot control its own currency cannot implement independent fiscal and monetary policies'.[88] Five Star also says it wants to renegotiate some of Italy's large public debt.

If anything, the Northern League has in the past been

even more hostile to the EU than Five Star. Its leader, Matteo Salvini, used a press conference the morning after the UK's Brexit vote to call for a change to Italian law to allow a referendum on Italy's own exit from the EU.[89] He has led a public 'Basta Euro!' (Enough of the euro!) campaign. In interviews in the late summer of 2017 he talked about giving Europe 'one last chance', a change in tone described by *Libero*, an Italian daily that expounds views close to those of the League, as 'a small shift in foreign policy from Euro-nihilism to Euro-scepticism'.[90] And in addition to campaigning successfully for greater autonomy for the northern Italian regions of Lombardy and Veneto, he has ridden the Northern League into third place in the polls on the back of strong anti-immigrant rhetoric. He is a strong opponent of the Schengen Agreement.

The Northern League does not necessarily face Five Star's challenge of trying to win alone since it has previously served in coalition with others on the right of Italian politics and may do so again. Its most likely path to power is in a coalition with Silvio Berlusconi's Forza Italia party, alongside which it successfully fought elections in Sicily in November 2017. However, while it has previously been a junior partner in a Berlusconi-led government, any new coalition would, the polls suggest, be a much more evenly matched affair because the Northern League and Forza Italia appear to have similar levels of support. And since Berlusconi is also barred from holding the top job again due to a fraud conviction, Matteo Salvini could emerge as an Italian Prime Minister.[91] Berlusconi has also taken up a strong anti-euro tone of late, suggesting the adoption of a double currency, with the euro used for international transactions and the old Italian lira being reintroduced internally.[92]

The centre-left Democratic Party may yet stage a spectacular comeback, some entirely new pro-European force could emerge in Italian politics in the vein of Macron, or Forza Italia and the Democratic Party could attempt some form of grand coalition. Absent one of those developments, however, a Eurosceptic breakthrough of one kind or another in Italy may soon be with us. A head of steam for a change to Italy's relationship with Europe appears to be building. If and when it comes, no one could say the warning signs were not there and, as I will argue in the next chapter, the exit of a country like Italy or France would set in train a series of events that would destroy the EU as a whole.

Trigger 4: Secessionist nationalism

Another possible trigger for EU collapse could come out of a secessionist crisis. Here, the recent and ongoing challenge of Catalonia ought to be instructive. Since the crisis broke there has been speculation about the possibility of political contagion to other parts of Europe. In the UK, many Scots seek independence and would surely be emboldened in their campaign for it if a nation like Catalonia were to succeed in achieving recognised statehood in Europe. In Belgium, both Flanders and Wallonia flirt with the idea of separation, leaving some to speculate that Brussels may end up as an independent city-state. In Italy, the Northern League is agitating for greater autonomy. So worried is former French Prime Minister Manuel Valls that he has argued Catalan independence could be the end of Europe. And Jean-Claude Juncker, in similar vein, has speculated on how unworkable the EU would become if it was made up of ninety-eight possible entities rather than the current twenty-eight (and down to twenty-seven once the UK leaves). This threat of political contagion should be taken seriously.

But the threat to Europe does not come only from political contagion. At the height of the Catalan crisis the Spanish finance minister, Luis de Guindos, warned Catalonia that if it went independent it would suffer a 'brutal pauperisation'. He talked of a reduction in Catalonia's GDP of between 25 and 30 per cent, an unemployment rate that would double, and the expulsion of Catalonia from the euro. Any new currency it introduced, he went on, would be devalued almost immediately by at least 50 per cent.[93]

There are two interesting points to note about this. First, should it ever come to pass it may well have seismic ramifications for the whole of Europe. Catalonia is the richest part of Spain and makes up around a fifth of the Spanish economy.

With this fifth gone, Spain's debt-to-GDP ratio before Catalan secession of around 100 per cent would increase to around 120 per cent. That debt would have to be serviced by the remaining, and poorer, parts of Spain, which themselves would most likely be in a slump due to the scale of disturbance secession had caused to the whole of the economy. In this scenario, in which secession is accompanied by a major dislocation of economic activity between Catalonia and the rest of Spain, there would also be little hope of the Catalans agreeing to shoulder their part of the debt, which would be impossible anyway with an independent Catalonia now outside the euro. There would instead be a good chance that markets would become deeply sceptical of Spain's ability to service its large debt. The Bank of Spain acknowledged the link in late September 2017, saying that if tensions worsened further, 'it would initially affect Spain's sovereign risk rating and afterwards spread through other interest rates'. A Spanish sovereign debt crisis might therefore be the result. As interest rates on Spanish government bonds went through the roof, the context could be created for Spain to need a bail-out from its European partners. Given the size of the Spanish economy, existing bail-out funds might not be enough and the conditions attached to them might in any case be unacceptable to the Spanish public. Spain has barely begun to recover the ground it lost amid the devastating effects of the last crisis, and its political system has become fragmented and volatile.

Amid this kind of turmoil in Spain, markets would demand to know who or what ultimately stood behind the country and its debts. This would be a toxic question to answer in many other European countries, especially in Germany, where the idea of German taxpayers providing bail-outs to southern European countries who appear to have mismanaged their own affairs remains an unpopular one. Neither the willingness to lend nor the willingness of Spain's citizens to meet the conditions attached to any borrowing could be guaranteed, and Spain might be driven to insolvency and an exit from the euro as the only means of escape.

The second point to note about this entire scenario, however, is that the economic damage would be the result of political choices. The dislocation of economic activity between Catalonia and the rest of Spain would not occur as the result of some inevitable economic logic. The warnings issued to Catalan leaders about the economic effects of independence were not predictions, but threats. They were the economic dimensions to a strategy that saw politically motivated arrests of Catalan politicians and activists and wider attempts to supress the Catalan separatist movement. The EU's own chosen policy position on the Catalan crisis is also not without significant problems. Formally, it has adopted a strategy of non-intervention in the internal affairs of Spain, while making it clear that Catalan independence would not be recognised and an independent Catalan state could not therefore become part of the EU. It took a similar, though not identical, approach to the issue of Scottish membership of the EU during the referendum over Scotland's independence in 2014. In what many saw as an attempt to influence the outcome, it said an independent Scotland would not be able to remain in the EU but would have to apply for membership, possibly going to the back of a queue of others still wishing to join.

The danger in this stance is that the EU is positioning itself as a defender of the status quo in a continent demanding change. And the demand for that change is not, in itself, illogical or always bad. In fact, the argument for separation can be quite compelling precisely because the EU, and the single market in particular, exists. Separation, if recognised by the EU and its existing members, does not in principle have to mean the end of access to a large domestic market. Smaller states are also treated well in some EU institutions. On the governing council of the ECB, for example, the central bank of each member state has exactly one vote, no matter how large or small the state is, so why would a region like Catalonia not see some advantage in going it alone? Its influence in the EU would almost certainly increase. Arguments that some states are not large enough to be viable are also not credible, given that Malta is a member, with a population of 420,000, which is about a third of the population of the English city of Sheffield. Similarly Estonia could fit into

London, in population terms, about seven times over. And it is not as though separation is without precedent. Belgium used to be part of the Netherlands. Since the end of the Cold War, we have seen the break-up of Yugoslavia, Czechoslovakia and the Soviet Union. And new or re-emerged states such as Croatia, Slovenia, Estonia, Latvia and Lithuania have gone on to be admitted to the EU.[94]

The real EU position seems to be that separatism is acceptable, just not in states that are already members of the European Union. And while the structures and institutions of the EU in some ways encourage it, demands for it in specific cases are actively discouraged. This is not a recipe for stability. Indeed, it could be a recipe for disaster. Many secessionist movements have traditionally harboured goodwill towards the EU. But it now runs the risk of being seen as a barrier to the legitimate aspirations to independence of secessionist peoples and movements across Europe. Since these movements are an increasingly evident feature of European politics, the EU could be on the path to losing further legitimacy in the eyes of many whose loyalty and goodwill it needs to retain. Whether through a contagion process that produces an unmanageable number of entities in Europe, the wider economic consequences of a disastrous attempt to punish separatism inside a major member state, or an ill-advised attempt to defend the status quo at the European level that produces an anti-EU backlash, the politics of secession in Europe could well trigger the unravelling of the euro and the collapse into disorder of the EU.

Trigger 5: The breakdown of the Turkey–EU migrant deal

Another possible trigger for the break-up of the EU nests in its troubled diplomatic relationship with Turkey. There are compelling reasons why the EU and Turkey should cooperate. The EU accounts for about half of Turkey's total trade and Turkey is the EU's fourth largest trade partner behind China, the US and Russia.[95] Turkey is an important NATO ally of most EU member states and an important player in efforts to deal with the situation in Syria, including in the effort to deal with Islamic State terror. The deal between the EU and Turkey on migrants is therefore only one dimension of a relationship that carries real diplomatic significance and weight. Nevertheless, speculation that the deal could collapse has been almost continuous ever since it was signed. The diplomatic relationship is fraught. Both the Erdoğan government in Ankara and many politicians in the EU see political advantage in confrontation. For Erdoğan, it allows him to claim the EU is not interested in a close relationship with Turkey and Turkey need therefore pay little heed to what the EU says on matters of democracy or economic reform. It provides him, in short, with political cover for his ongoing efforts to remodel the country in his AKP party's image. Some politicians in the EU, on the other hand, use a tough line on Turkey to pander to concerns that Europe may be overrun by Muslims and lose its Christian identity.

Specific tensions about the migrant and refugee deal also exist. In September 2017, Ömer Çelik, Turkey's Europe minister, told the *Financial Times* that Turkey had honoured the promises it made in the agreement but the EU had not done the same, either with regard to the promised €3 billion in aid for the three million refugees in Turkey, or on visa liberalisation for Turks wishing to travel in Europe. He also complained at a lack of progress on the opening of new chapters in Turkey's negotiation to eventually become a member of the EU.[96] For these reasons and others, the talk on the Turkish side from time to time has been of the deal being newly 'evaluated'. The EU has vigorously rejected the Turkish account of what it has done under the terms of the deal. It claims almost a billion euros was paid out in refugee aid to Turkey by mid-2017 and that the rest of the promised €3 billion was dispersed by the end of the year. But even it doesn't argue that things are going well. Evidence of a small number of ISIS terrorists passing through Turkey to Europe means progress on visa-free travel is highly unlikely. More widely, ever since the attempted coup in Turkey in July 2016 and the crackdown that followed it, EU leaders and officials have accused Ankara of a massive erosion of democracy and the undermining of both human rights and the rule of law. Jean-Claude Juncker has talked of Turkey taking massive strides away from Europe. And in the middle of a German election debate with SPD leader Martin Schulz in September 2017, Chancellor Merkel declared openly that Turkey should not become a member of the EU. This prompted Çelik to unleash a 25-tweet tirade in which he accused German leaders of spreading 'evil' while fanning the flames of populism. To all intents and purposes EU entry talks with Ankara are dead and at the time of writing discussions about enhancing Turkey's relationship with the EU customs union were suspended.

The tensions both in the diplomatic relationship in general and on the migrant deal in particular are therefore clear and the political incentives are not all stacked in favour of an improvement. The current relationship is not stable enough to be taken for granted. It could yet get much worse, bringing down the migrant and refugee deal with it.

This has to be a worry not only because the chances of it happening are not negligible but also because the underlying conditions that are driving large numbers of migrants and refugees to travel north and west to Europe from Africa, the Middle East and central Asia are not changing for the better. If the Turkey–EU deal does break down, we can expect migrant and refugee flows to the EU to shoot back up, with very serious consequences. The first point to note about this is that the breakdown of the deal, unless accompanied by a major new effort by EU countries to meet the challenge collectively, would yet again expose the divisions between them. At the end of 2017, the deal was still to some extent shielding those divisions from public scrutiny. Without it, they will be back in full view. Since one of the key arguments in favour of the EU is that it is only by acting together, at scale, that many of the challenges of the twenty-first century can be met, this would be deeply damaging to the EU's standing and to perceptions of its effectiveness. Migration would once again be seen as a poster-child for EU failure.

We can also expect in any deal breakdown scenario that borders inside the EU's Schengen zone would be reintroduced. The Schengen regime might not be formally killed off, because it does allow for the temporary reintroduction of border measures in some circumstances. To all practical intents and purposes, however, it would cease to function as individual EU member states engaged in unilateral action or acted in small groups to end unrestricted free movement across the zone. The significance of this cannot be overestimated. A close adviser to Chancellor Merkel told Mark Leonard, the head of the European Council on Foreign Relations (ECFR), in late 2017 that 'the EU could survive another euro crisis, but not another migration crisis, because open borders are part of the constitutional foundation of the EU – if EU borders close, it will be the end of the EU'.[97] Neither is this just about symbolism. If migration flows increase significantly and borders inside Europe go back up, a political dynamic is likely to be unleashed that would be extremely threatening to the EU's continued existence. If the Leave vote in the UK can see a boost in polls of around 5 per cent by milking the issue, the warning is clear. A new migration crisis would be a boon to Eurosceptic political movements around the continent. In countries like Italy, Austria and France, where the populist and Eurosceptic vote is already strong, this could be enough to propel such forces to victory and to trigger exits from both the euro and the EU.

If past evidence is anything to go by, the political damage will also not be confined to the countries receiving the most migrants and refugees. Public attitudes to open borders in the Schengen area are heavily impacted by concerns about security threats and fear of the unknown. A report by the ECFR in 2016 was instructive on this point. It noted:

> In Lithuania, which received 275 asylum applications in 2015, a poll found over 80 per cent of the population believed that refugees may contribute to a rising level of crime and social unrest. In Estonia, where 225 people applied for asylum … 59 per cent of the population is ready to give up the Schengen agreement to reduce perceived threats related to uncontrolled refugee flows.[98]

The reintroduction of borders in the Schengen zone could also be expected to have serious economic consequences.

There are around 1.3 billion cross-border trips and some 57 million trucks carrying €2.8 trillion worth of goods within the zone annually. If border controls were permanently reintroduced, some estimates suggest cross-border trade within the zone could be reduced by 10–20 per cent over the long term. The reintroduction of borders would also deter cross-border employment, limit job opportunities and restrict the supply of labour to employers. Growth would also be reduced, leaving the zone with a GDP almost 1 per cent lower than otherwise might be the case by 2025.[99]

In the context of EU economies growing at around 2 per cent a year and a general economic outlook that looks positive, these impacts may not be hugely significant. If they were to take place in conditions of much lower and even no economic growth, however, they could be one factor among several contributing to a further life-threatening recession for the EU. Whether via a powerful stimulus to further EU division, a boost to Eurosceptic political forces or a blow to the economies of the EU, there are clear and plausible paths from the breakdown of the EU–Turkey migrant deal to the more fundamental breakdown of the EU.

Trigger 6: Macron's drive for a fiscal union backfires
It is presumably the existence of trigger scenarios like those already outlined in this chapter that has Emmanuel Macron so worried. He has intervened in the debate about the future

of Europe in a forceful way since becoming President of France and his motivation for doing so couldn't be clearer. In his visionary speech at the Sorbonne in September 2017, he described the continent as in a state of budgetary, financial and political civil war, where the door had been left open to nationalists and populists by the complacency of a political class and citizenry that had taken the EU for granted. Amen to that.

At the heart of Macron's proposals on how to respond was the call for a fiscal union, comprising a stronger common budget, mostly paid for out of some common European taxes. The budget should, as noted earlier, be under the control of a single European minister and subject to strict European Parliament control. Its creation, he argued, would provide stability in the face of economic shocks, since 'no state could face an economic crisis alone when it no longer controls its monetary policy'. To make the common budget politically palatable, along with the effective transfers from wealthier parts of Europe to poorer parts that it would entail, Macron declared that all members of the eurozone would have to take increased responsibility for observing the rules collectively designed and set by themselves. And all would need to implement essential reforms to prevent them being a lag on growth while helping Europe compete with the United States and China.

Here, then, was a call for the kind of fiscal union that many believe is essential if the single currency is to survive. Buried in the proposal is the idea that when recession or trouble hits one part of the eurozone, tax revenues from another can be used to smooth demand, absorb the shock, and buy time for adjustment. In this sense, it is a bold proposal with a clear economic logic. The problem is that whereas reforms in other areas have been vague or timid precisely so as not to provoke the toxic politics associated with one part of Europe 'bailing out' or helping another, this set of proposals seeks to take on and win the argument for that kind of redistribution from first principles. It is needed, Macron argues, as a show of solidarity. It is about unity and cohesion, without which the EU can never be strong.

One can admire Macron's boldness while still acknowledging that there are clear risks accompanying this approach. The first and most likely is that Macron's proposals may fail to get backing from elsewhere on the continent. Along with the other remaining weaknesses in the institutional architecture of the euro described in Chapter 5, this arguably would leave the single currency in a weaker position than it was even before Macron was elected. Reforms that many perceive as essential to the long-term stability of the single currency would have been very publicly called for and failed to get traction. Markets may remain sanguine while the eurozone is undisturbed by shocks and continues to grow but in the event of trouble, a huge question mark would quickly hang over the extent to which the solidarity required to save it really exists.

The second and more politically explosive risk is that Macron may get traction for his proposals but that they stimulate a political backlash that has the effect of strengthening Eurosceptic populists across the continent. In some wealthier parts of Europe, the fear will be that the transfer of funds will remove the necessity for fundamental economic reform in the less wealthy areas and therefore will represent a case of good money being thrown after bad. In countries on the receiving end of expenditure from the proposed common European budget, suspicion will focus on any conditions attached to such expenditure and on precisely what Macron meant when he talked of 'increased responsibility from all'.

We can expect Eurosceptic populist movements to ruthlessly exploit such sentiments, in some cases portraying the common budget as a transfer from the harder-working parts of the continent to the lazy or corrupt. Measures designed to make the euro stronger economically may therefore provide ammunition to those looking to undermine support for it politically. There is also the possibility, even probability, that Germany will give Macron constant rhetorical support and some of what he wants but not on a scale sufficient to make the reform genuinely effective. To really perform the function of a shock-absorbing and stabilising measure for the eurozone, the common European budget is going to have to be very large. Too large for the German and some other publics to stomach. But a half-hearted implementation of what Macron is suggesting could prove to be the worst of both worlds. The toxic politics of transfers between nations could be triggered but the euro would remain vulnerable to shock when the next crisis came. The opponents of the euro would then be able to tell voters that everything has been tried to save it and that the problem with the single currency is not that it is weak institutionally but flawed irretrievably. The only way forward is therefore to leave it.

The fear that a fiscal union might be suggested but fail to gain support may explain why Macron's predecessors were reluctant to embrace the fiscal union concept with any great gusto, and may lead some to conclude that Macron has ultimately been unwise to do so as publicly and effusively as he has. The fear that a fiscal union may actually be attempted and fail the test set for it when a crisis comes should be a concern of equal or greater standing. Either way, the great new hope of European reform, President Macron, may have triggered slow-burning political dynamics that ultimately sow the seeds of the eurozone's destruction. He may simply have shone a light on the fact that the political solidarity required to make fiscal union, and the single currency, work does not exist.

The trigger scenarios considered in this chapter do not exhaust the plausible ways in which the EU could be pushed from crisis to the edge of collapse. One could add others, such as an act of super-terrorism like the detonation of an Islamist dirty bomb in a major European city, that could have the same effect. But one has to stop somewhere. One of the most frightening things for supporters of the EU to contemplate is that some or all of the triggers just discussed, and others beside them, could occur alongside and even feed off each other. Disintegration by perfect storm is not out of the question. To survive, the EU needs a lot to go right and only some of this to go wrong. Whatever the trigger, my contention is that events such as these would unravel the Union as a whole. It is to the mechanisms by which this would happen, and to the likely consequences on the continent of Europe in terms of economics, politics, and security and geopolitics, that I turn next.

CHAPTER 7

THE ECONOMY FROM TRIGGER TO COLLAPSE

M ost of the trigger events just discussed point to the possibility of one or more major country exits from the single currency. Eurosceptic politicians in favour of euro exit claim it could be carried out smoothly and without, in Marine Le Pen's words, 'breaking the dishes'. But is this really the case? In this chapter, I take a look at what a euro exit process might look like and examine why, far from being a smooth process, it would trigger not just the break-up of the eurozone but the break-up of the EU as we know it, with dire economic consequences.

It would be one thing if exits from the euro came about as a result of all members of the single currency collectively deciding to unravel it. Technically and politically, that would still be extremely challenging but at least in that scenario the participants could count on it being attempted as a cooperative endeavour. It is so unlikely, however, given that no member states currently favour that as a course of action, that it is not worth seriously considering. If euro exits happen, they will come via one of two other possible routes. The first involves a state choosing to leave of its own accord. The second involves a country being forced out by the markets under a cloud of speculation about its inability to repay its debts. In practice, these two would be impossible to separate, since a decision to leave the euro by one major country will trigger contagion dynamics that result in one or more other states being effectively forced out too. To understand why, it is necessary to think about the process by which an initial exit might unfold.

In the case of a state choosing to leave of its own accord, its people would presumably debate the merits of exiting the single currency for a prescribed period of time before deciding, via a vote, whether or not to do so. This is clearly the process envisaged by a wide variety of Eurosceptic politicians, from Le Pen and Mélenchon in France to Salvini and Di Maio in Italy. They may suggest trying to avoid euro exit through a process of fundamental renegotiation of relations with the EU first, but if that fails, their preference is for putting the issue to the people in a national plebiscite. If such a vote said yes to euro exit, the country concerned would then presumably set a future target date for implementation and would get on with the necessary planning, and printing and distribution of the new national currency to be (re)introduced. On the set target date, a redenomination of all monetary values from euros to, say, the franc would take place.

An understanding of what would happen next is critical to one's assessment of the chances of this being a smooth process. Even in this example of a smooth exit, once introduced the franc would almost certainly be instantly devalued against the euro and other major world currencies. This devaluation would occur partly because the new currency would lack credibility as a store of value, and partly because of the uncertain economic outlook in the country introducing it. However, the devaluation would be expected and presumably seen as a benefit by the government leading its country to the euro exit door, since one of the reasons why the government in question would be choosing to introduce a new currency in the first place would be to allow just such a devaluation to happen. It can't take place inside the euro but should, so the thinking goes, increase the competitiveness of the leaving country's exports. The hope would be that, as a result, growth would return or be boosted over time, especially if the government chose to use its post-exit monetary policy freedoms to help boost demand. In the short term, however, even in this scenario there would almost certainly be a recession due to economic uncertainty impacting negatively on levels of investment, imported inflation, and weak domestic demand brought on by domestic wages being held down. If wages were not held down, the gain in competitiveness sought through the combination of introducing a new currency and its devaluation would not materialise and any supposed benefits from leaving the euro would be vastly outweighed by the pain.[100]

As part of an orderly process of leaving the euro, and in order to prevent capital flight, capital controls would need to be introduced in the exiting country, at least for a time. Marine Le Pen acknowledged this might be required during the French presidential election campaign in 2017 while playing down its significance and suggesting that it would only be for a few days. The logic pointing to the need for capital controls is clear: if the franc is going to be worth less than the euro at a specified date in future, why leave your euros in French banks to be redenominated into francs and devalued at that future date if you can move your money into euro accounts elsewhere before that happens and preserve the value of your money? Introducing capital controls would not necessarily even violate the European treaties. Theoretically, Article 59 of the Lisbon Treaty could be used to introduce capital controls while staying within the bounds of treaty commitments, provided a qualified majority vote of other EU members agreed with the idea.

Some default on debts would almost certainly be part of this managed exit process. Some of this would be domestic, some international. Again, the logic is simple: the recession would drive some institutions and individuals in the exiting country into bankruptcy and their debts would therefore go unpaid. Those individuals and companies with debts in euros or other international currencies who were now being paid in devalued francs would also find it harder to meet their international debt obligations. Banks would be hard hit since the recession at home would leave them with more bad loans while the relative cost of repaying international loans would increase. Some of the effects would just have to fall where they might. In an orderly, managed process of the kind envisaged by politicians like Le Pen, however, the government would step in to help at home, and abroad some of the bigger impacts on debtors and creditors would be subject to international negotiation. While such negotiations would be difficult, the argument would be that with goodwill on all sides, agreement might be possible. Could it be, then, that the Eurosceptic political leaders who promote euro exit as a solution to their country's woes are actually on to something, and that even though their countries would have to endure short-term pain, warnings of chaos and doom on the back of leaving the single currency are greatly exaggerated?

The answer is no. If we rewind this exit scenario back to its start point and think through what other actors would be doing at each stage of the process, another picture begins to emerge. One reason why it is hard if not impossible to see any scenario playing out in the way just described is that the entire timetable would be massively condensed by market sentiment and reaction. Rather than a smooth and sequential process of national political debate, vote and new currency implementation, people would begin moving their money immediately an exit looked possible. The process timetable would collapse and its many challenges would have to be managed simultaneously and at high speed rather than sequentially and over a longer time period.

Let's assume that a Eurosceptic government in a country like France or Italy came to power and that its attempts to renegotiate its relationship with the EU had failed. If true to their word, they would then put exiting the euro, or the EU as a whole, to the people in a referendum. Let's also assume that in a country that had recently elected a Eurosceptic government, a vote to remain in the single currency could not be taken for granted. Even the act of announcing that negotiations had failed and that a referendum was to be held might be enough to trigger market panic. But absent that, every twist and turn in the opinion polls would be watched by savers and investors with assets in the country as they tried to gauge the extent to which their assets were at risk. In a vote that was too close to call or one in which polls were leaning towards exit, there would be capital flight, a run on the banks, a nose-dive in economic activity, a collapse in the price of the leaving government's bonds and a spike in yields demanded by anyone left willing to provide debt finance to the government in question. This could all be expected *before the vote had even taken place* and none of it would be a surprise. In Greece, some €150 billion left the banking system during the crisis there, amid widespread runs on the banks and even, on occasion, violence outside them.[101]

Since the last crisis, moreover, European banks have more than doubled their holdings of their own governments' bonds, from €355 billion in 2008 to around €800 billion by late 2016.[102] As the leaving government's bond prices collapsed, the balance sheets of their own banks would take a hammering. Since those banks also have no regulatory requirement to hold capital against sovereign bonds the losses would force many banks into insolvency. Even if the bond price collapse didn't do it alone, other developments would help the process along. The impending redenomination and devaluation would leave the banks and other corporate entities in the exiting country unable to borrow because lenders would not be confident they would ever be paid back. Widespread concern over liquidity and solvency risks would also dry up credit. A wave of corporate and banking insolvencies would result. The public finances of the exiting country would deteriorate rapidly and the chaos and devaluation that would take place before, during and after exit would therefore also quickly leave that country unable to refinance or service its debts. The default to follow would not be just any default. A major country exit from the euro would represent the biggest sovereign debt default in history. In 2017, there was an estimated €1.7 trillion of French public debt issued under French law. By comparison, the restructuring of some of Greece's sovereign debt to private creditors in 2011/12 covered only around €200 billion. A major country exit would make Greek default look minuscule by comparison. The exiting government could try to ignore new European Banking Union rules to announce that it was using taxpayers' money to stand behind the banks but given the difficulties it would be experiencing on the debt markets it would quickly find itself unable to make good on that promise within the euro.

Contagion to the rest of the eurozone would be inevitable. First, institutions elsewhere in the eurozone would suffer real and heavy losses, since European banks and non-banking financial institutions are still substantially exposed to the sovereign and commercial debt of other eurozone countries. *Die Welt* reported in July 2016 for example, that French banks alone were exposed to Italian debt to the tune of €250 billion.[103] Second, the sight of a core member of the eurozone leaving would cause speculation that others would follow. A collapse in the value of bonds issued by other eurozone governments would occur, especially but not only those issued in the eurozone periphery. Again, many of the domestic banks holding their own government bonds would be forced into insolvency. Taxpayers in these countries would once again be on the hook to bail out the banks because collective eurozone procedures and mechanisms would quickly be overwhelmed. The doom loop linking government and bank debts would have returned. But this time, right from the off governments would lack credibility in attempting bail-outs since debt-to-GDP ratios have in many cases still not recovered from the last crisis and are too high even before further bail-outs are attempted. The belief that other countries were about to be forced out of the eurozone would also curtail credit to their banks and commercial entities. The jurisdictions experiencing capital flight would grow larger, further triggering waves of business insolvency, bank collapse and deteriorating public finances.

Other areas of the core of the eurozone would find themselves massively affected. Italy's banks, as noted in the last chapter, could not handle a credit event of this scale triggered either at home or elsewhere in the eurozone. And many in Germany would come to understand that, as Wolfgang Munchau has pointed out, 'a massive current account surplus has its downsides. There is a lot of German wealth waiting to be defaulted on.'[104] The event, in fact, would be global. Despite attempts to reform the international financial system since the last crisis, one of its key vulnerabilities remains its opacity. Few people believe they can really be sure of who owes what to whom. Amid the crisis that a major euro exit would represent, not only the real costs of a massive default but also fear of the unknown would drive a widespread seizing up of credit, leading to further insolvencies and chaos. A major country exit from the euro would, in short, represent 'probably the most violent shock in history, dwarfing the Lehman Brothers bankruptcy in 2008 and the 1929 Wall Street Crash'.[105]

The question would then be: how might the eurozone institutions seek to respond? It is worth examining this question, first in relation to the exiting country that has triggered the process and second in relation to the rest of the eurozone as a whole.

As just described, the exiting country would be going through a major crisis. Under normal circumstances, the European Stability Mechanism might be used to provide a bail-out to the government in question, and the bail-in rule anticipated in the Banking Union would be used to help resolve some of the failing banks. The Single Resolution Fund would also be used to help recapitalise them and the ECB could step in to provide liquidity assistance. In the case of a major country attempting to leave the euro, however, none of this prescribed crisis management practice could be expected. Any and all of these measures would represent help to a country that had provoked the crisis itself and was looking to leave the single currency anyway. It would be provision of support with no conditions attached because none could be enforced. And it would be help to a country that would no doubt go on to use devaluation of its new currency as a tool to seize market share and undercut jobs in some of the countries providing the support. To describe assistance from the rest of the eurozone as a tough sell to voters doesn't even begin to capture the political challenge encapsulated in efforts to mount a response. And in any case, the exiting country would be unlikely to accept help even if it was on offer.

More devious eurozone leaders might see a political opportunity in inaction. As noted in Chapter 2, at the high-point of the last euro crisis the ECB showed itself willing to use its control of liquidity support to troubled countries' banks as a tool to leverage decisions it wanted out of their national governments. It threatened first to cut off liquidity to enforce the prioritisation of private creditor interests in places like Greece, and then later, in Cyprus, it used the same threat to force the government there to engage in a bail-in. Some might think that in withholding support now, the ECB could demonstrate to an exiting country that even contemplating a euro exit brought nothing but chaos. The hope might be that a dramatic fall in public support for exit during this chaotic process would cause an exiting country's government to suspend the process and look for a face-saving way of abandoning exit altogether.

If this strategy were attempted, it too would almost certainly fail. An elected Eurosceptic government might well choose the other available option. Instead of abandoning the referendum and exit process, it would almost certainly try to curtail the chaos by speeding it up. It would try to execute a referendum at only a few days' notice, if it felt confident it could win. More ambitiously, it might even abandon the idea of a vote altogether and try to execute the exit itself in a matter of a few days. If this was done on a Friday evening, the entire redenomination process could take place over a weekend. Citizens and institutions would have euros in their bank accounts at the close of business on Friday and francs, for example, on Monday morning. Depending on whether the move brought not just devaluation but also stability to the exchange rate in a reasonably short period of time, capital flight might continue for a time but then subside. Many of the losses likely to fall on investors and savers would become a fait accompli. A Eurosceptic government pursuing this course of action could even claim its recent election victory had provided it with a sufficient mandate to respond to market chaos in this way. It could claim it had not anticipated such events or intended such actions but given the circumstances, the national interest dictated such a course.

Unable to either prop up the exiting country or to do anything to stop its exit, inaction would most likely characterise the European response. The eurozone would have to cut the exiting country free while trying to manage the consequences. In the longer term the eurozone's hopes would rest on the exiting country becoming a spectacular economic failure, while its fears would be that it became a strong post-exit success. As a report on the subject of a euro exit by Capital Economics in 2012 made clear:

> If the devaluation and default [associated with leaving] failed to provide a boost and the country remained mired in chaos and depression, then public opinion in the peripheral countries would surely line up behind whatever tough measures needed to be enacted domestically ... But suppose a success was made of euro exit. Suppose that the exiting country managed to repeat what Argentina achieved after 2002, with growth surging and unemployment falling. In that case, it would surely be impossible for politicians in the peripheral countries to argue that there was no alternative to never-ending austerity within the euro.[106]

In the short term, however, all European attention would have to be focused on how to manage contagion. In approaching this, it seems clear that no pre-existing mechanisms in the eurozone's locker would be sufficient to deal with the crisis. Despite all the efforts to strengthen the architecture of the euro in recent years, its institutions and mechanisms would be overwhelmed. The European Stability Mechanism has not been built to handle crises in economies the size of France, Italy or Spain let alone in a number of them at the same time in a contagion scenario. The Banking Union is inadequate and would be politically unworkable. There is no way that a banking crisis on this scale could be responded to entirely through use of bank resolutions and bail-ins. Italy, as previously discussed, has already shown itself unwilling to use such tools in the case of much smaller crises anyway, and has opted for taxpayer funded bail-outs instead, so as not to hurt the millions of smaller retail investors who would lose otherwise. In France, more than 40 per cent of government debt is held by French savers, pension funds and institutions, who would suffer massive losses in a bail-in. They would of course be hurt by redenomination, devaluation and bail-out under the reintroduced franc but a bail-in would be far worse. And bail-in via sovereign debt write-off or restructuring would also wipe out the French social security system, which is mostly invested in sovereign bonds.[107]

The ECB, for its part, would be in an extremely exposed position. In recent years, it has lent many eurozone banks money at low interest rates while taking some of the sovereign debt held by those banks as collateral. Much of the lending has been to banks in peripheral or weaker economies in the EU like Portugal, Ireland, Spain, Greece and Italy. There were two worthwhile purposes to these loans. First, they were designed to take illiquid assets like sovereign bonds of questionable value off the balance sheets of banks and replace them with cash that could more easily be lent to businesses and citizens in the real economy. Second, they were designed to provide demand for eurozone peripheral country sovereign bonds, to thereby prevent a collapse of the value of those bonds and an increase in the interest rate that governments issuing them would have to pay. Worthwhile or not, the upshot, from the ECB point of view, is that the bank is now heavily exposed to eurozone periphery sovereign debt. If a country leaves the single currency and triggers the kinds of events described above, the ECB can be expected to suffer very heavy losses. Precisely how much would depend on which country or countries were exiting and how much their governments and banks defaulted on loans. Much of the collateral accepted against those loans would be rendered worthless in a context in which one or more major sovereign defaults were occurring and many of the loans on the ECB's books might have to be written off. Though many economists argue that central banks cannot go bankrupt because they can simply print more money, that argument is not as clear-cut as that. The ECB could effectively go broke.[108]

To stop contagion, eurozone leaders would therefore have to reach for something bolder and bigger than any measures previously contemplated. Theoretically they could look to turn national debts into common European debts by issuing Eurobonds. They could also try to massively increase the funds available to the European Stability Mechanism. This would be to make clear to the markets once and for all that the eurozone would not be allowed to unravel and that its members would stand together. To put it another way, it would be an attempt to arrest contagion by making clear that the taxpayers of the wealthier eurozone countries were ultimately willing to stand behind the debts of the poorer. The ECB could complement this with liquidity assistance to Europe's banks, though in a system-wide crisis, the scales of support required would be massive. The Greek banking system became chronically dependent on such assistance at the height of the Grexit crisis and assistance peaked there at around €124 billion of support in 2012. In a country like France alone, however, bank deposits are more in the region of €4 trillion.[109] In addition, the ECB could reverse the taper of its quantitative easing measures to bolster the market for European sovereign debt.

The comment pages of Europe's newspapers would certainly fill up with a debate on the requirement for some or all of these measures to be introduced. There would be a powerful economic rationale for going down this road. Failure to do so might, after all, condemn the euro to the dustbin of history. For this reason, there are many people in Europe who automatically assume that if finally backed into such a corner, Germany and other wealthier countries in the eurozone would ultimately do what was required because it would be in their own economic interests to do so. The problem with this assumption is that it ignores politics. Measures like the mutualisation of debt and the provision of liquidity assistance on a massive scale would require not only a complete reversal of Chancellor Merkel's position but also the abandonment of the mindset that has dominated German economic and public thinking on the eurozone for years. It would require not just an economic and political shift but also a psychological one. The debate on a massive injection of additional funds to the ESM would also once again trigger the toxic interstate politics of debt that was so corrosive to European solidarity in the last crisis. Additional public support needed to provide the money in some countries would need to be matched by a willingness to accept the conditions attached in others. To say such conditions would be unpopular is an understatement. Even if Merkel or another German Chancellor attempted this strategy to save the euro, it is highly unlikely that the governing coalition could survive without the need to fight another election, an election that it might not win. The same is true also of other creditor countries in the euro area.

Moreover, the political chaos and uncertain support surrounding such a strategy would itself potentially undermine the intended market-stabilising effect of declaring that Eurobonds were to be introduced. Markets could not be sure that there would, in the end, be follow-through. And if in trying to win the argument for them and other measures, the claim was made that bailed-out countries would be subject to severe economic restraint in return for help, then the 'help' itself would trigger movements to leave the euro in peripheral countries that could stomach no more austerity. In both the eurozone core and the periphery there would be a powerful perception that the euro was a never-ending problem that it would be better to leave behind.

There is every chance the German elite in particular would find it politically more viable to cut the periphery loose and try to preserve a smaller eurozone of core countries that shared its economic outlook, not because they preferred this outcome but because this was the only viable choice other than losing the eurozone altogether. It seems to me that this is true whether the route to exit had been via a Eurosceptic party coming to power and triggering the process voluntarily or whether a political crisis such as that in Catalonia had triggered economic chaos sufficient to force a country like Spain to the exit door. When dealing with the larger eurozone economies, an exit would challenge the German leadership in particular to choose between everything they have so far resisted and led their public never to expect, and what might be perceived as the lesser evil of allowing some to leave the euro while trying to maintain a shared currency with others.

It therefore seems clear that a major country exit from

the euro would trigger a series of events leading to the wider unravelling of the eurozone itself, at least as currently constituted. And were that to happen, a further series of consequences would be likely to follow. There would be serious ramifications for the European economy as a whole. Output would fall. There is a good chance that the payments system underpinning intra-eurozone trade would collapse. The single market would fragment and effectively cease to exist, and free movement of people would also most likely end.

The historical data on the economic consequences that flow from the disintegration of currency unions makes for sober reading. The three other European examples of currency zone break-up of most significance are those of the Habsburg Empire, the Soviet Union and Yugoslavia. They are imperfect cases against which to assess the possible effects of a break-up of the eurozone but that does not mean that nothing of relevance can be learned from them. In his treatment of the history of these cases, Anders Åslund of the Peterson Institute for International Economics notes that the output falls associated with the switch away from a shared currency were huge:

Officially, the average output fall in the former Soviet Union was 52 per cent, and in the Baltic States [then part of the Soviet Union] it amounted to 42 per cent. According to the World Bank, in 2010, five out of twelve post-Soviet countries

– Ukraine, Moldova, Georgia, Kyrgyzstan, and Tajikistan – had still not reached their 1990 GDP per capita levels in purchasing power parities. Similarly, out of seven Yugoslav successor states, at least Serbia and Montenegro, and probably Kosovo and Bosnia-Herzegovina, had not exceeded their 1990 GDP per capita levels in purchasing power parities two decades later.[110]

The causes of these output falls were many, as Åslund contends, not least the consequences of the change from communist systems to market economies and, in some cases, war. But even after controlling for such factors Åslund estimates the additional hit from the move away from a shared currency was something in the region of 20–25 per cent of national output. He is far from alone in his view. A study for ING in 2011 explicitly examined what the impact of eurozone break-up might be.[111] It anticipated a fall in output in the eurozone area as a whole of between 5 and 9 per cent in the first year, and between 9 and 14 per cent over three years. In other words, 'a deep recession across the eurozone … dragging down the global economy'. Neighbouring countries outside the eurozone would also be seriously affected. The projected impact on the UK, for example, was for a fall of 3 per cent in output.

A contributing factor, and one which might in fact put these numbers on the optimistic side, is likely to be a crisis in the eurozone's TARGET2 payments system. When the eurozone was created its design did not involve the creation of one unified central bank and the disappearance of all national central banks. On the contrary, the old national central banks remain in existence and sit alongside the ECB, acting in many ways like its national branches in the different member states. To facilitate payments between eurozone countries, commercial banks in member states maintain deposit accounts with their own national central bank. When a payment is required between say, a company in Spain and one in Germany, the Spanish company's bank informs the Banco de España that the payment is necessary. The Banco de España then deducts the deposit account it holds in that bank's name by the required amount and instructs the Bundesbank to add an equivalent amount to the Bundesbank deposit account of the commercial bank working for the receiving company in Germany. That commercial bank then adds it to its own client's account. No money changes hands; a number of euros are effectively withdrawn from circulation in Spain and the same number are created in Germany.

The TARGET2 payment system is both the electronic plumbing that makes all this possible and the ledger that keeps track of the total flow of payments. Prior to the financial crisis of 2007–08, the system was more or less in balance as flows between countries largely balanced each other out. Since then, substantial imbalances have frequently been evident. These have occurred for a number of reasons, some of which can be illustrated by persisting with the Spanish–German example just mentioned. Prior to the financial crisis, the Spanish company might have borrowed money from a commercial bank in Germany to pay its German supplier. The TARGET2 system would have been balanced, because the loan from Germany to Spain would have appeared as a flow in one direction and the subsequent payment from the Spanish company to its German supplier would have appeared as a flow of the same size in the other. At the height of the financial crisis, however, as commercial banks stopped lending to each other and to their commercial clients, many companies in the southern periphery of Europe, including Spain, had to borrow from their own national banks rather than from a commercial bank in another part of the eurozone to maintain their activity. In TARGET2, our example would therefore show up as a flow out of Spain without a compensating flow back in or, to put it another way, as a case of the Bundesbank issuing euros at Spanish request in Germany without the Banco de España issuing any balancing euros at German request in Spain. Given trade imbalances within the eurozone, with the southern periphery running current account deficits and Germany and several others in northern Europe running current surpluses, it is no surprise that this situation quickly produced large TARGET2 imbalances. The system continues to function because it is based on trust. The Bundesbank continues to issue euros to its German commercial clients at Spanish request on the theoretical understanding that at some point in future, all account imbalances in the ledger will be settled.

In a scenario in which a euro-exiting country made clear it was defaulting on its TARGET2 obligations, that trust would be shattered. And in an exit contagion scenario there would be uncertainty as to whether others might follow. Contagion could flow through the plumbing of TARGET2, leading countries to stop trusting the system and to the breakdown of the payments system itself. Member countries would have to settle their trading bills with each other with the hard assets, such as currency reserves, in their possession. Since some of the deficit countries are not rich in hard assets and would find it virtually impossible to borrow on the markets in such circumstances, the almost certain consequence would be a breakdown in intra-eurozone trade, a deep euro-zone-wide recession and possibly depression, and a massive increase in unemployment not only in deficit countries but in surplus countries too. Effectively, the oil that keeps the intra-eurozone trade engine turning smoothly would run dry and that engine would seize up as a result.

The way European countries trade with each other in a eurozone collapse scenario would also be heavily impacted by knock-on effects on the functioning of the single market. That market is not just a legal framework but a network of production and supply relationships spanning the continent. Businesses have taken the stability provided by the single market as a green light to invest across the continent and to integrate deeply with partners in other parts of Europe. Much trade is now not in finished products but in components that move backwards and forwards across national frontiers in complex and integrated pan-European supply chains. These networks drive competitiveness and efficiency into more parts of Europe than otherwise would be the case and they result in technology being shared and productivity increasing.

If the euro unravelled, this pattern of behaviour and its beneficial effects would be thrown into reverse. A full collapse would mean up to nineteen new currencies would be introduced. In a throwback to the 1970s, there would be great monetary and exchange rate instability in Europe and consequently a major increase both in exchange rate risk and in insurance premiums for those who wanted to protect against it. Businesses would be highly likely to refocus investment and activity back to domestic markets, so at the business level, the single market would begin to fragment.

The damage would also be done at policy level. The relative value of newly introduced currencies on open markets would fluctuate considerably. Some would depreciate in value very quickly and some, like a reintroduced Deutschmark, would appreciate. Some countries would enjoy a boost to their competitiveness as a result of currency devaluation while others might see an increase in unemployment. The former Irish Prime Minister John Bruton has argued that 'exports would become dramatically uncompetitive in some cases, and in others they would become so cheap that there would be accusations of dumping and currency manipulation'.[112] In similar analysis for the European Council on Foreign Relations, Sebastian Dullien has argued:

> Calls for new non-tariff barriers for trade, capital controls, or new subsidies for ailing industries could be expected to follow soon. As the break-up of the eurozone would almost certainly entail balance of payments difficulties for at least some member states, at least some of these actions would even be legal under Article 144 of the Treaty on the Functioning of the European Union, which stipulates that EU member states may take unilateral action to protect their balance of payments even if these restrictions damage the single market.[113]

Such measures, if imposed, would effectively end the single market not only as a series of functioning business networks but also as a single legal and economic space.

Elsewhere in the architecture of European institutions and regimes, the Schengen Agreement would also come under significant pressure. Given that much of Europe would be suffering from a deep recession, and that unemployment would be rising, it is highly likely that migration flows would increase from those parts of the continent doing very badly to those doing better. The presence of increased numbers of migrants would be politically explosive in receiving countries and could easily stoke a new wave of xenophobia. This could be expected to fuel support for nationalist parties but in the short term, the policy response would likely be to introduce controls over free movement of people. New barriers to entry and border checks would be introduced and some would inevitably seek to suspend the Schengen Agreement or formally pull out of it altogether.

We would then be living in a Europe in which both the single currency and single market had dissolved or substantially shrunk to a core around Germany, a huge recession had created massive unemployment, and intra-eurozone labour migration had undermined the political viability of free movement. Trade would be restricted due to new trade barriers, increased exchange rate risk and the collapse of the TARGET2 payment system. Whether anyone stood up and formally declared the EU dead or not, dead is what it would be. The economic consequences for Europe as a whole would be dire. A new phase in European history would commence. What might we expect of its politics?

CHAPTER 8

POLITICS AFTER THE EUROPEAN UNION

The European Union is not, of course, only an economic union. It is a political union as well, organised around a publicly declared and shared set of values. These values are captured in Article 2 of the Treaty on European Union, which reads as follows:

> The Union is founded on the values of respect for human dignity, freedom, democracy, equality, the rule of law and respect for human rights, including the rights of persons belonging to minorities. These values are common to the Member States in a society in which pluralism, non-discrimination, tolerance, justice, solidarity and equality between women and men prevail.[114]

In a Europe after the European Union, it is my contention that these values will be attacked more aggressively and systematically than at any time since the 1930s. If the last chapter is right in arguing that a collapse of the euro would, by its very nature, be a disorderly and chaotic process with hugely damaging economic consequences, we have to ask what impact that chaos would have on European politics.

While there are many who would be deeply saddened, even angered, by the EU's collapse, it is hard to construct scenarios in which the supporters of a liberal, open, tolerant and cooperative Europe would be its beneficiaries. Even if more liberal forces were eventually able to regroup, they would be unlikely to reassert ideological or political dominance for many years into the future. The chaos of collapse would destroy the credibility of the elite that presided over its onset. The validity of the values they spent years describing as foundational to their approach would be subject to far harsher scrutiny. And the cessation of cooperation, at least temporarily, would serve as a rebuke to all those claiming that international cooperation was essential to future progress. The collapse of the EU would therefore be a historic defeat not only for the idea of European integration and cooperation but for a Europe of pluralistic governing institutions, serving a society built on the primacy of individual freedom.

Even before a collapse, these values are already under visible strain. MPs in a Council of Europe committee passed a resolution in September 2017 warning of a crisis of commitment to democratic values across eastern and central Europe and in some of the countries wishing to join the EU in future. Their warning focused on attacks on the separation of powers, efforts to limit the legislative powers of elected parliaments and the pervasive influence of corruption. Countries including Poland, Hungary, Bulgaria, Romania and Turkey were all named as culprits.[115] A closer look at some of them makes it easy to see why.

In Hungary, the Orbán government has cracked down on independent organisations, attacked freedom of the press, and restricted the independence of the judiciary. Emblematic of the assault has been the regime's attempt to close down the Central European University, an independent entity funded by Hungarian émigré George Soros, with the aim of helping to cultivate leadership commitment to the values of an open society. Poland's Law and Justice Party, in power since 2015, has pursued a similar course, interfering with the judiciary and the independent media. Protest in Poland is no longer guaranteed to come without persecution, and when it takes place it is not always in defence of the democratic principles enshrined after the collapse of communism. The offices of women's campaign groups have been raided by police for no other reason than that they played a role in organising demonstrations against a new anti-abortion law. And in November 2017, a march organised by far-right groups drew tens of thousands to the centre of Warsaw.

Some tried to dismiss the latter as nothing more than a celebration of Poland's national day, but the reality was something far more sinister. Co-organised by the National Radical Camp (ONR), the march attracted far-right groups from across Europe, including Italian fascists from the Forza Nuova group and supporters of the Jobbik party in Hungary. The ONR's aims are to preserve Poland's ethnic homogeneity. The march's other co-organisers, the All-Polish Youth, describe themselves as a group of 'racial separatists'. The event itself kicked off with chants of 'Smash, smash, smash liberalism; our way is nationalism'.[116] Speakers included Roberto Fiore, an Italian fascist who reportedly has close links to the British National Party and who is said to have fled Italy in 1980 to avoid the Italian police. He was wanted at the time for questioning with regard to a bombing in Bologna railway station that had killed eighty-five people.[117] The response of Robert Bąkiewicz to accusations of fascism is also interesting. One of the organisers of the Warsaw demonstration, he spends no time straining for respectability through a denial of basic anti-liberal sentiment. He contests the 'fascist' label, but only because he says he prefers instead to be described as an authoritarian.

Perhaps it should surprise us that members of Poland's Law and Justice Party have been regular attendees at this now annual event, and that the event has on occasion opened with a welcome letter read out on behalf of Poland's

President, Andrzej Duda. The reality, however, is that even with the EU in existence and with Poland a signatory to the Treaty on European Union and its Article 2 statement of values, the norms of acceptable public opinion are changing. Through demonstrations such as this, and the actions of the Polish government, illiberal authoritarianism is being made respectable again. There have, of course, been counter-demonstrations against what the government is doing, but for any non-Pole who has read of the tragedy visited upon Poland by both fascism and communism in the twentieth century, or who has spent a gut-wrenching day at a venue like the museum of the Warsaw Rising, what is going on today can be hard to comprehend. Surely here, so soon after the end of Soviet occupation and a new flowering of democracy, there would be no space for a new authoritarian politics? Sadly, this is precisely where we are.

Elsewhere in Europe, the presence of growing intolerance and xenophobia is also clear. Targeted at migrants and refugees, it is underpinned by a political-cultural Islamophobia that is becoming rife. Again, far from being hidden from respectable view, it is increasingly flaunted openly. Zoltán Kovács, press spokesman to Prime Minister Orbán in Hungary, has backed up his boss's claim of a Muslim invasion of Europe with the firm assertion that all Orbán is trying to do is to preserve European heritage. 'European culture is based on Christianity, like it or not,' he says. 'Our vision is to maintain the original cultural environment in which Europe has flourished. We want to stay as we are – a Christian continent.'[118] The Muslims, by definition, are not welcome.

The EU, to be fair to it, has been trying to defend its core values against attack. Article 7 of the Treaty on European Union provides a mechanism for it to do so. It contains a safeguard against reversion to authoritarian rule in an EU member state, and was introduced in 1999 specifically to handle the prospect of the EU taking in post-communist countries then undergoing transition. Under the terms of the article, four fifths of the EU's members in the Council of Ministers can determine that there is 'a risk of a serious breach by a Member State of the values referred to in Article 2'.[119] They can do so if such a motion is proposed by a third of members of the Council, or by the European Parliament or Commission. And if such a serious and persistent breach is agreed, the Council of Ministers can suspend the EU voting rights of the country in question.

The Commission and European Parliament have been inching in this direction. The Commission concluded in 2016, for example, that the Polish government's effort to control the country's Constitutional Tribunal was a threat to the rule of law. Later, as the authorities in Warsaw sought to extend their control over other courts, Frans Timmermans, the European Commission vice president with responsibility for fundamental rights and the rule of law, declared that the changes proposed would 'abolish any remaining judicial independence ... because judges will serve at the pleasure of political leaders and be dependent upon them from their appointment to their pension'.[120] The European Parliament has further expressed its view that events in Poland represent 'a danger to democracy, human rights and the rule of law'. And Hungary has not escaped either. The Commission has taken the Hungarian government to court over its attempts to curtail minority rights and NGO freedoms.

Article 7 has not been invoked but the Commission is close to trying to invoke it. In practice, however, politics and precedent make it hard for it to do so. The formalities of the process, as just described, are tortuous. To finally agree that the values enshrined in Article 2 of the Treaty have been breached, all other members of the Council of Ministers have to unanimously agree that a member state is violating those values. Countries like Poland and Hungary can therefore effectively provide political cover and protection for one another's violations. There is also considerable reluctance to use Article 7 to its full potential because member states worry about precedents being set and whether such an article might one day be used against them. One can understand why Spain, for example, in view of its handling of the Catalan crisis, might not wish to throw its weight around accusing others of falling prey to undemocratic behaviour. The high salience of migration and terrorism in European politics has also made many governments determined to use judicial and restrictive measures that in other circumstances may be perceived as running counter to EU values. This makes them reluctant to take too fundamentalist an approach on the invocation of Article 7 in relation to the behaviour of others. And then there is the concern that actually triggering Article 7 could backfire, contributing to a surge of anti-EU sentiment in any country facing its sanctions.

All that said, the EU's existence and the presence of the Article 7 threat have combined with residues of popular support for the EU in places such as Poland and Hungary to complicate life for the illiberal governments there. And to its credit, recent actions by the European Commission have served to shine a light on emerging authoritarian practices, placing a modicum of restraint on the governments engaging in them. Were the EU to collapse altogether, the pressure and restraint currently being applied, albeit weakly, to countries violating its values would disappear and the residual commitment to those values in some governments may well disappear with it. Indeed, in the context of an unmanaged unravelling of the EU's economic order such as that described in the last chapter, not only would restraints on illiberal authoritarianism be removed but it is highly likely that every facet of the authoritarian project would be given a massive boost.

In that scenario, economic conditions would quickly become dire. The challenge of migration would not have disappeared, driven as it is by deep underlying factors like conflict, poverty and the effects of climate change in the EU's southern and eastern neighbourhoods. Russian support for Eurosceptic, nationalist and authoritarian movements would, if anything, intensify. The social pain of economic disarray would not be spread evenly but, as in the last crisis, it is the poor who would suffer the most. Something, and someone, would have to be blamed for the state of crisis. With liberal political forces and elites in disarray, the politics of post-EU Europe would be angry and the politicians most likely to thrive would be those most adept at giving anger a home.

We can expect scapegoating on a massive scale. Some of this would pit state against state and nation against nation. For a glimpse of this unwelcome tomorrow, look no further than some of the uglier episodes in Europe's recent past. At the height of the last euro crisis, the bitterness and historical antipathy that surfaced between Greece and Germany, for example, knew no bounds. One drawing by the popular Greek cartoonist Stathis Stavropoulos contained an onlooking German soldier, a row of gas chambers and a caption about Greek jobs being burnt. In one demonstration against austerity in Athens, a German flag was burnt outside the Parliament building. In another an actor dressed as Hitler, and a side-kick dressed as an SS officer, pretended to rape a woman said to represent Greece. One of the daily newspapers published a mocked-up photo of Angela Merkel wearing a swastika armband. And calls were heard for Germany to pay reparations to Greece for the appalling experience of wartime occupation in which an estimated 300,000 Greeks died of starvation. To link the past even more explicitly to what he perceived was happening in the present, cartoonist Stavropoulos put down his drawing pencil and opted for words: 'Germany', he said, 'has already tried twice to make Europe German. This time it's through economic means.'

Neither was the traffic all one way. The German media pandered to its own public's mood of resentment at the idea that Germany should pay for bail-outs of the Greek economy. Claims that the Greeks were lazy and unproductive were commonplace. *Focus*, a German magazine, ran a front cover describing the Greeks as 'the frauds of the EU', alongside a photo of the Venus de Milo statue wrapped in a torn Greek flag. Even senior government ministers, like former finance minister Wolfgang Schäuble, were injudicious with language, describing Greece at one point as a 'bottomless pit'.[121] The fact that much of the bail-out money was being used to help German banks that were overexposed to Greek debt hardly penetrated the public or political consciousness.

These parallel and hostile national media narratives fed off each other to heighten the tension. Every time *Bild*, the

German tabloid newspaper, published a headline like 'NEIN: not one more billion for the greedy Greeks' and encouraged its readers to post selfies with the same message, *Demokratia*, the Greek newspaper, would respond with two-page banner headlines with the retort 'Lies from *Bild* again!'[122]

If this could be viewed as tension born of a unique and painful history between two countries on a continent otherwise gratified by a historical legacy of harmony, it could, perhaps, be put down as an unfortunate but isolated episode. The problem for Europe is that beneath the rhetoric of EU solidarity and the claim that the continent has moved beyond the ugly politics of the twentieth century, it actually remains littered with national animosities, unsettled historical scores and deeply ingrained and often hostile stereotypes with the power to cause mayhem. If the EU unravels, jobs are lost and international debts are left unpaid, the blame will, as sure as night follows day, cross borders. It will be carried by a resurgent nationalism that digs at the graves of dormant but not forgotten national narratives and stereotypes – a kind of ideological necrophilia, lusting over the corpses of European politics, sustained by the claim that it and it alone knows where the bodies in this graveyard are buried.

The post-EU politics of antagonistic interstate relations will find one of its most powerful outlets in a new and bitter politics of trade. The continent will be characterised by claim and counter-claim as to who is using unfair practices to undercut the market share, jobs and wages of others. Europeans will no longer be partners in an effort to raise the labour standards of all, but will increasingly be told by politicians and the media to see each other as problematic foreigners to be blamed for worsening conditions. While the political centre-left, such as it still exists in Europe, struggles to prevent it, the populists of both left and right will pit worker against worker on national lines. Here, post-EU Europe will struggle to resist the sort of rhetoric unleashed elsewhere by Donald Trump. His language is blunt and bears little relation to economic reality but his narrative on unfair trade practices, currency manipulation, and the need for economic nationalism is both clear and politically effective.

A sample:

'They [Japan] have cars coming in by the millions, and we sell practically nothing. When Japan thinks we mean it, they'll stop playing around with the yen. They're almost as good as China.'

'We will keep the car industry in Michigan and we're going to bring car companies back to Michigan.'

'The devaluations of their currencies by China and Japan and many, many other countries, and we don't do it because we don't play the game.'

'Anybody we do business with beats us. We don't win at trade.'[123]

In the politics of post-EU Europe, we should expect all this and more. Protectionism will stalk the continent as the single market unravels. Tariff and non-tariff barriers, disintegrating employment and environmental standards, and the unravelling of intellectual property regimes are all extremely likely. The dynamic of these efforts to compete against rather than stand with each other is already present in the Europe of today, where repeated efforts by various member states to cut corporation tax rates to secure a bigger share of inward investment into the EU have been evident.[124] But it will be turbocharged if the EU collapses. Many of the populists in Europe already resort to Trump-like rhetoric. In the lee of the EU's collapse, they will be much freer to choose and name their targets. 'The French are taking us for idiots,' a populist from the Alternative für Deutschland might say. 'They are deliberately devaluing the franc to flood the German market while taking measures to keep us out of France. It is preposterous to suggest we should just take it. No one has anything against the French people but the interests of German workers and businesses must be pro-tected. And let's remember, what is made in France today can be made in Germany tomorrow, only better.' Elsewhere, an Italian from the Five Star Movement or Northern League will offer a salvo in the other direction. They might ask:

Who do the Germans think they are? For years, they had us locked into a single currency on terms that favoured them and almost no one else. They've grown fat while we have been crucified on a cross of euros. And now? Now that we have our own currency back and can compete more fairly, they shout about unfair trade practices, and do everything they can to keep us out.

Another target for scapegoating will be the domestic elites who led their countries into the EU and claimed they could make it work. The attack here will not only be on their competence but on their identity. The argument will be commonplace that those who led 'the people' into this mess are now using the international links and networks they built up while doing so to relocate themselves and their families to escape the carnage. Their mobility will be the hallmark of their disloyalty. The true people, it will be said, are being left to pick up the pieces. And in this distinction between the true people and the disloyal elites will be the roots of yet another dimension of post-EU political scape-goating. If solidarity with one's own people, defined presum-ably along ethnic, national or religious lines, is the ultimate test of loyalty, then those not seen as legitimate members of the community will be subject to exclusion. There will be a measure of respect and tolerance for those who belong. For the 'outsider', there will be no such thing.

Nowhere should we expect exclusion and intolerance to be more on show than in attitudes towards a rhetorically merged population of Muslims, refugees and migrants. The presence of, and vulnerability to, Islamophobia in Europe is already clear and undeniable. There is no practical reason why a Europe of twenty-eight member states could not have coped in 2015 with an influx of refugees and migrants smaller in number than those residing in Lebanon alone. The truth is rather that many of the member states of the EU didn't want to deal with the refugee and migration issue because those arriving were predominantly Muslim. This narrative, as has been noted, is explicit in some parts of central and eastern Europe that have Christian-nationalist governments, but even in the more liberal elites of western Europe the problem is widespread and deeper than many find it comfortable to admit. The best that can be said for many, especially in what might be called the mainstream centre-right, is that they prefer not to acknowledge Islamophobia as a problem. More worryingly, there are many who prefer instead to pander more to the views of those stoking fear and public anxiety about Muslims in the first place. The response to any kind of negative incident involving Muslims, migrants or refugees is instructive. Writing about a German example in *Foreign Affairs* in 2016, Alexander Betts noted the following:

Statistically there is no greater likelihood that refugees will be involved in terrorism or crime than the general populations. But perception matters. Germany's open immigration experiment is clearly under threat from a familiar pattern: a negative incident occurs that implicates refugees, the media pounces, the far right mobilizes, and the centre-right shifts inches closer toward tightening borders.[125]

Even in today's better economic circumstances, with the eurozone growing more strongly than for many years, European political leaders have failed to construct a narrative for their populations about how best to think about Islam in Europe. They have too often allowed terms like 'refugee', 'migrant', 'terrorist' and 'criminal' to be conflated. And policies have been introduced across the continent that undermine the liberal values the EU is supposed to reflect and champion. If Europe stands for anything it ought to be for individual freedom. It is that belief that underpins the concern for human rights, freedom of speech, religion and association, democracy and gender equality. All the harder to reconcile, then, with events in places like Bornheim, Germany, where authorities responded to reports of sexual assault by banning *all* adult male refugees from swimming pools. Hard too to reconcile with asylum seekers in Cardiff, Wales, being forced to wear coloured wrist-bands which mark them out from the general population.[126]

If that is the picture in relatively good times, now imagine what will become acceptable once the EU, the bogeyman to be blamed for migration policies that are too soft and do not work, is gone. It is not that Muslims will be blamed for the downfall of the EU, unless it is an Islamist act of super-terrorism that triggers the process of disintegration, but that the gloves will be off with regard to policies on refugees, migrants and the social integration of Muslims. In post-EU Europe, multiculturalism, already on life support, will be dead. Refugee deportations will be just another tool of policy, whatever the international conventions say. On borders, the scene will be chilling. The dream of a borderless continent will be replaced by a Europe of barking dogs, roaming searchlights and barbed-wire fences.

Exclusive identity politics is likely to be so powerful for psychological as well as ideological reasons. Europe after the European Union will be a continent in shock. Since it will not only be the EU itself that has been swept aside but the ideas it represented and the political, economic and media pundits who supported it, there will be a powerful sense of dislocation. It will not just be markets and institutions that disintegrate but much of the mental furniture that has sustained them. As one era ends there will be huge uncertainty about what could and should replace it, and both an ideological and psychological void that the politics of scapegoating will be well primed to fill. Agreeing that a variety of outsiders and disloyal elites are to blame for the crisis will provide a form of social glue. Welding the new system together will be claims that elites and migrants are 'twins who thrive off one another. Neither is like "us", both steal and rob from the honest majority, neither pays the taxes that it should pay, and both are indifferent to local traditions'.[127] Such will be the nature of a powerful reactionary response to the deep psychological need for order in what otherwise will appear to be an enveloping sea of chaos.

Ivan Krastev has captured this well in the context of his writing about the utility of conspiracy theories in contemporary Polish politics. The governing Law and Justice Party, he argues, has been effective at building support by using the accusation that Russia deliberately caused the death by plane crash of former President Lech Kaczyński in 2010. Krastev says:

> Scholars tend to argue that such [conspiracy] theories are most popular during periods of major social change and that they represent a desire for order in a complex and confusing world. But what is happening in Poland today has revealed something more: how, in some cases, a shared belief in a particular conspiracy theory can play a role previously reserved for religion, ethnicity, or well-articulated ideology. It can be a marker of political identity ... It consolidates a certain 'we'.[128]

This climate of post-EU European politics will not be consistent with the maintenance of pluralistic governing institutions. The attack on them will commence with grave-side commentary on why the EU failed in the first place. From the ashes of shared sovereignty to the dust of the EU's economic treaties, the entire edifice will be subject to post-humous reputation assassination. The collapse of the EU will be taken by those welcoming its demise as confirmation that the pooling of sovereignty does not, and cannot, work. This, alongside the attempt in EU treaties to constitutionalise basic economic decisions like what size of budget deficit and levels of public debt a state should run, will be said to have placed power beyond the reach of voters and to have ripped the guts out of national political debate. Not for nothing did the Brexit campaigners run their insurgency around the mantra of taking back control. But we should not expect the subject of the EU to disappear from political discourse. A constant nationalist and sovereigntist effort to ridicule what it repre-sented will be an important part of the ongoing struggle for ideological dominance in post-EU Europe.

And power redistribution from European to national level will be only one feature of an intense post-EU politics of constitutional reform. The attack on power sharing and pluralistic institutions will have a strong domestic dimen-sion too. For populist insurgents the shipping of power to the EU abroad and the ineffective separation of powers at home are but two sides of the same flawed constitutional coin. They have together, the claim will be made, formed a system in which power has been so widely dispersed as to make it almost impossible to ever get anything done. Claims of powerlessness while in office, in fact, will be identified as part of the smoke-screen that has been used so successfully by mainstream politicians for so long either to justify their inability to solve real people's problems, or to mask their lack of desire to do so.

The answer, it will be argued, must be to not only take back control from Brussels but to concentrate more domestic power in the hands of strong national leaders who can then wield it to deliver decisive change in the interests of 'true Poles', 'true Hungarians' and others. The politics of post-EU Europe will witness an attack on the very idea of the separation of powers that liberals believe is essential to democratic health. There will be little to stand in the way of absolute power corrupting absolutely.

Tactically, the politics of scapegoating and the drive to concentrate power will be married to appeals to direct democracy through extensive use of referendums. Here Viktor Orbán in Hungary has again shown the way. This is how he justified his anti-migrant referendum against the idea of an EU quota for resettling refugees and migrants across the continent:

The government believes that democracy is one of Europe's core values, and the European Union is also based on the foundations of democracy. This means that we may not adopt decisions – those that significantly change people's lives and also determine the lives of future generations – over the heads of the people, and against the will of the European people. The quotas would redraw the ethnic, cultural, and religious map of Europe. The Hungarian government takes the view that neither the EU, nor Brussels, nor the leaders of Europe have the authority to do this.[129]

The question he put to the Hungarian people on this basis was this: 'Do you want the European Union to be able to order the mandatory settlement of non-Hungarian citizens in Hungary without parliament's consent?' Orbán then demonstrated his passionate commitment to the flowering of democracy in Europe by spending billions of forints on a massive campaign of lies about migrants. Against the backdrop of an EU request that Hungary take in only 1,294 asylum seekers, an eighteen-page government booklet mailed to 4.1 million households in Hungary declared that 'forced settlement endangers our culture and traditions'. Asylum seekers and migrants were linked to increased terrorism. Voters were falsely told that in other major European cities such as London, Paris and Berlin, whole neighbourhoods full of migrants had become no-go areas for law enforcement authorities. And across the country, government sponsored billboards asked questions such as:

Did you know that Brussels wants to settle a city's worth of illegal immigrants in Hungary? Did you know that since the beginning of the immigration crisis the harassment of women has risen sharply in Europe? Did you know that since the beginning of the immigration crisis, more than 300 people have died as a result of terror attacks in Europe? And, did you know that close to one million immigrants want to come to Europe from Libya alone?[130]

This was no referendum carried out to ascertain the views of the people. It was a referendum conducted precisely because the regime already knew the views of the people and wanted to demonstrate what they were to opponents at home and around the world. The campaign was a vicious mobilisation of pre-existing anti-immigrant sentiment dressed up as an exercise in popular consultation. In a post-EU Europe, much more of this can be expected. Referendums, far from being vehicles for inclusion in a more participatory and de-centralised form of democratic decision making, will be a powerful weapon wielded to delegitimise minority opinion and to justify majoritarian rule.

And what will this dystopia born of Eurosceptic dreams deliver with regard to the capacity for Europeans to cooperate with each other? Not surprisingly, the ideological climate will be incapable of underpinning cooperative European endeavour on matters affecting all of us. The ongoing roll-back of the single market, the toxic politics of debt default and trade, the shuttering of borders in place of Schengen, all this will dominate over any efforts amid the chaos to construct new forms of cooperation. We should expect some of the effects of loss of multilateral capacity to be functional, but the causes will partly also be down to changing diplomatic culture and practice.

Some of what the illiberal authoritarians are doing in Europe today is already eroding the ability of EU governments to work together. When countries are as integrated as they have become in the EU, they rely on each other to fulfil commitments and to apply legal frameworks without systematic political manipulation and bias. For as long as the Union has been bound together by a shared set of values the members have been willing to assume this was the case and to operate largely on the basis of trust. The daily operation of dozens of committees, Commission meetings and European parliamentary sessions has also provided the glue of strong interpersonal relations across national boundaries.

If the EU unravels and collapses that event will represent the biggest unwinding of Europeans' trust in and commitment to one another in decades. It will end the intensity of daily diplomatic engagement that EU membership has required and cultivated. And it will sap the capacity of Europeans to work together, both because they will find it much harder to agree on common goals and action in the first place and because they will lose the diplomatic habit and practice of doing so effectively even when they can.

The consequence will be to damage Europe's prospects further. The European voice in climate change negotiations will be shattered and its constructive influence to date in pursuit of a low-carbon future massively diminished. The same can be expected on matters of trade. The single biggest point of leverage the EU has on global trade talks is its ability to control access to the European single market. If that market no longer exists, even large European countries like Germany will find themselves not at the dinner table of trade talks but effectively on the menu. China and the US will run the show. Closer to home, the collapse of the EU in chaotic and divisive circumstances will mean it is gone as a pole of attraction for those in the Balkans and other parts of the European periphery. This will impact not only the dream of membership but levels of commitment to the model of governance that EU membership would have required. For countries already plagued by corruption and still limited democratic tradition, the fall of the EU will increase the chance of them succumbing, in turn, to authoritarianism. More widely, Europe's ability to collectively export a kind of stability to the Middle East, north Africa and eastern Europe, such as it is, will give way to the unmanaged import of national and collective instability.

For those who believe the sheer ineffectiveness and

unpleasantness of what is likely to follow the EU will serve to prevent its demise, there is this warning: it is easier to explain Brexit as the vote of an island people always half distant from Europe than it is to explain how Donald Trump ended up in the White House. The EU is vulnerable to collapse today in the same way that the US presidency was vulnerable to populist capture. Neither is there any guarantee that the problems of governing that follow a turn in this direction will persuade people of the need for a quick return to 'normality'. If the EU falls, Europe fragments and the politics of scapegoating takes hold, every subsequent governing reverse has the potential not to undermine the new order, but to reinforce the narrative that led to it in the first place. The outsiders and foreigners are to blame. Tough action against them is the answer. Even peace in a Europe after the EU cannot be taken for granted, because the end of the EU won't just undermine the capacity for European cooperation, it could trigger the dynamic that leads the continent back to conflict.

CHAPTER 9

SHATTERED PEACE?

The political conditions just described are likely to be reinforced by what would quickly become the deteriorating security environment of post-EU Europe. The EU's Security Union will be destroyed by the wider process of break-up. Islands of cooperation will remain but as cross-border intelligence and information-sharing practices ebb, the tasks of countering terrorism, managing borders and dealing with the trafficking of small arms and people will all become harder. Europe will likely import more crime, instability and terror and the effects will be visible in rising violence on our streets and in our cities. If the terrorists score some big and, in their terms, spectacular victories this will have major political consequences. European publics are only human. They will be willing to tolerate ever more radical measures in the attempt to deal with what they perceive to be the unprecedented level of threat. And in an environment in which liberal values are already in retreat, the effect may well be to smooth the path to intolerance and the erosion of civil liberties while legitimising the development of more extensive surveillance states across much of Europe. Given the power of current and emerging digital technologies to assist with this process, and their potential reach over many aspects of day-to-day life and communication, the consequences could be frightening.

THE END OF NATO TOO?

The collapse of the EU would have massive geopolitical consequences. For much of the period since the end of the 1940s, western Europe has seen power politics progressively constrained by a web of voluntarily negotiated multilateral treaties and legal obligations.[131] These have not only facilitated a long period of stability but over time they have come to provide a source of moral authority. They have offered a sense that Europe had somehow learned from the disastrous experience of unconstrained power politics in its past and had found a better, more civilised way forward – a model, many felt, for the rest of the world to follow, not least because for a long period of time, it appeared to be successful. Some even speculated that the EU would come to run the twenty-first century, an age ripe for lawfare rather than warfare.[132]

The collapse of the EU would not only challenge but reverse all that. It would represent a change to both the structure and the process of international relations on the continent of Europe and the change would not be for the better. For one thing, it is hard to see how the North Atlantic Treaty Organisation (NATO), Europe's only really effective collective security organisation, could survive such a momentous development. Its European membership is almost identical to that of the EU. On a continent with the single market unravelling, trade barriers and border fences going up, potential competitive currency devaluations taking place, and both very high levels of unemployment and the politics of cross-border scapegoating taking hold, how likely is it that the publics of Europe would be inclined to commit to each other's defence? How likely is it that their political leaders would see electoral advantage in continuing to argue for it? While no one might declare NATO dead in the formal sense (though this too could not be entirely ruled out), it would be clear to any potential adversary that the solidarity required to make its collective security guarantee credible no longer existed. Questions about solidarity are frequently asked anyway, and as discussed earlier, there is suspicion about whether some allies could really be relied on in a crisis. The management of this concern takes up a lot of time inside the alliance and is one of the reasons why NATO has found it difficult to engage with Russia in recent years, even as the relationship with it has deteriorated and at a time when more engagement might have been both desirable and beneficial. The worry, especially of those on the NATO–Russia border, is that NATO members in the south and west of Europe want dialogue at any price, and whatever the pattern of Russia's aggressive behaviour. It is but a short step, in their view, from dialogue to sell-out. We also know that some of the Eurosceptic politicians who might be influential in a post-EU scenario have negative views with regard to NATO. A Eurosceptic breakthrough in a major European state could lead that state to a NATO exit.

Whether disbanded in the formal sense and via proactive political choice or simply allowed to atrophy to the point of irrelevance amid intra-European economic confrontation and its consequences, an EU collapse will have a profoundly negative impact on NATO. The potential consequences of economic stress for defence and security relations were well understood by the original drafters of the North Atlantic Treaty. In the aftermath of depression and economic chaos in the 1920s and 1930s, and of the Second World War, they went to the trouble of committing in Article 2 of the treaty to working together to preserve economic harmony. They declared they would 'seek to eliminate conflict in their international economic policies and to encourage economic collaboration between any or all of them'.[133] In the language and spirit of the treaty, the unravelling of the EU would be nothing short of an attack on the economic foundations of peace in Europe.

NATO, of course, includes the United States. In pre-Trump days, the US could have been counted on to do everything in its power to make sure NATO survived a seismic shift like the end of the EU, and countries like the UK and Germany could be expected to try to compensate for its collapse with an effort to make NATO stronger. Since Donald Trump's election, however, none of this instinctive reaction either in Europe or the United States can be taken for granted. And without US leadership, attempts to strengthen NATO from the European side would lack credibility anyway.

Even before Trump, the level of US commitment to Europe was waning. The pivot or rebalancing to Asia led by President Obama was a clear reminder to Europeans that the US is a Pacific as well as an Atlantic power. And with the rise of China and massive economic development elsewhere in the Asia-Pacific region, few would doubt that the focus of the US in the twenty-first century must increasingly be on that side of the world rather than on this. The truth is that the security concerns that dominate in Washington today are not centred on Europe. For several years now, I have had the opportunity to test this proposition myself, working with a group of former political, military and dip-lomatic leaders to try to push Europe's security challenges up the political agenda in Washington. That effort has met with little progress, not least because the minds of policy-makers there are more consumed with the implications of

China's growing military power, the struggle for influence throughout the Asia-Pacific region between the US and China, and challenges like the nuclear programme in North Korea. Elsewhere Iran, Afghanistan and ISIS top the list of American concerns.

And as noted in the opening chapter of this book, US policy in places like the Middle East is actually likely to create more problems for Europeans, not less. To Europe's south, Trump is likely to inflame a region already in flames. In doing so, he will further divide Europeans as they come under pressure to support some of what he does. And in the background the collapse of the EU, if it happens, will worsen the increasingly poisonous debate over transatlantic burden sharing.[134] In the midst of a post-EU economic crisis, with increased welfare demands being placed on already overstretched national budgets, many European defence budgets will be cut. The Americans will notice. Some in Europe will no doubt buck this trend, seeing an opportunity to pursue a form of military Keynesianism, where increased public investment in defence both burnishes the credentials of nationalist leaders and helps meet the desperate need for new jobs to replace those being lost in the downturn.[135] But even in these cases the problem may not be the money so much as what the money buys. One consequence of EU collapse will be the continuation of inefficient patterns of national expenditure on personnel rather than deployable military equipment. In post-EU Europe, defence budgets will be pork barrel budgets and the queue of regions and interests seeking to benefit from them will be long. National-scale research and development efforts will persist largely in their current form, and even if the budgets are increased in nominal terms, they will remain too small to keep many European forces at the cutting edge of military technology. And those modest efforts at collective EU defence activity that already exist are almost certain to be killed off as part of the wider unravelling.

In Europe after the EU, we may see some increased bilateral collaboration between certain countries but there is no reason to believe it will be strategically significant in terms of Europe's total ability to defend itself.[136] Overall, we can expect a collapse of the EU to weaken not only the solidarity of Europeans with each other but also their capacity to defend each other without US help, even if they wanted to. In a Pacific century and in the age of Trump, this could be fatally corrosive to the US defence commitment to Europe as a whole. Perhaps Trump would pick one or two European states that he saw as deserving of reaffirmed US commitments in the form of new bilateral defence treaties. If he did so, these treaties would likely come at a price. We could expect the political solidarity of the North Atlantic Treaty and the collective security guarantee that saw western Europe through the Cold War to be replaced by a patchwork protection racket where the US defence shield was offered more robustly in some places than in others but only in return for both money and concessions on trade.

WHAT WOULD REPLACE
THE EU AND NATO?

If the old structure provided by the EU and possibly NATO was gone, what could be expected to replace it? The answer to this partly depends on just how the EU's collapse occurred, and on the choices made by political leaders especially in the Franco-German core of the EU. In the event that the euro disintegrated, Germany would have a choice to make. It could either go it alone with a reintroduced Deutschmark or it could try to salvage a small eurozone core in partnership with some of the countries in northern Europe whose economic attitudes and attributes most closely match its own. The latter might hold out the prospect of a little more economic stability and the preservation of what would effectively be a larger home market for German products and services. It might not, however, be acceptable to voters in Germany, or for that matter, to voters in the other countries, who would become subordinate players in a German-dominated economic zone. Inside Germany, voters might conclude that the common currency idea has been shown to be a major mistake and that preserving it, even in smaller and more cohesive form, would be to ask for more trouble further down the line. Elsewhere, more than one Scandinavian and Nordic politician told me during the writing of this book that, in the event that the EU does collapse, the smaller countries in that region would rather pursue deeper Nordic cooperation than accept such a German-dominated outcome. In structural terms, what can be said is that whether Germany is alone or is leading a smaller central/northern European bloc, it would become a crucial pole of power and influence in a multipolar post-EU Europe.

Further west, France would have to decide whether to act alone or try to become the leading nation in a southern European or 'Club Med' bloc. This could draw on the strand of thinking advanced by Nicolas Sarkozy in the French presidential election in 2007, and which subsequently played a role in the creation of the Mediterranean Union (MU). Sarkozy's vision was that the MU would be modelled on the EU with both common institutions and a shared judicial area. He even went as far as to suggest membership of it could be an alternative to EU membership for Turkey. The MU now exists, but only as a pale imitation of the EU in both role and influence. In a post-EU Europe, it is highly unlikely to be either the platform or the inspiration for a successful French leadership initiative, not least because its putative southern European members' economic interests are not aligned. Even if something new did emerge, it would not involve anything like the degree of integration furnished by the EU, nor a shared currency, but would be a much looser arrangement. More likely is that France too would act alone and seek to lead, from time to time, more ad hoc forms of European cooperation on specific issues. The southern European periphery would be unlikely to take on any structural form and identity other than that provided by the existing nation-states in the region, namely Spain, Italy, Greece and Portugal.

Elsewhere on the continent, the UK has already voted to leave the EU and would once again face the challenge, as it has at other times in its history, of how to use the remaining power and influence at its disposal to shape events in Europe from the sidelines. So far, it has failed utterly to articulate a strategy towards the affairs of the continent that would kick in after Brexit and is totally consumed with the process of Brexit itself.[137]

Turkey's role would most likely increase. It is already seeking to grow its footprint in the Balkans and could be expected to ramp up that effort to ensure the region does not become dominated by others, principally Russia and Germany. However, the big winner in the new geopolitical landscape is likely to be Russia. It has perceived a strategic interest in ridding Europe of NATO and of driving a wedge between its European members and the United States for decades. It has been more willing to tolerate the EU up to a point but over the last decade especially it appears also to have decided that the EU is a threat to Russian interests in eastern Europe. With the EU gone, Russia's relative power position will be enhanced and it will perceive, as a consequence, that it has a much freer hand.

And then there is the new role to be played by China. In late November 2017, a summit of what is known as the 16+1 took place in Budapest. This involved China (the one) and all the ex-communist countries of central and eastern Europe, some of which are in the EU and some not. Among the EU members at the table were Hungary, Bulgaria, Romania, Poland, Croatia, Slovenia, the Czech Republic, Slovakia, Lithuania, Latvia and Estonia. Matters such as national procurement rules, which are core EU competencies, were on the agenda, as was Chinese investment. China is now providing some of the capital needed to finance power stations, railways, roads, canals and other infrastructure that central and eastern Europe needs. Since 2012, that investment has amounted to around US$15 billion. This is still small compared to the size of current EU structural funds provided to the region, which amounted to €80 billion for Poland alone in the 2014–2020 EU budget round, but it is nonetheless significant. Were the EU to collapse and the structural funds to disappear, the importance of Chinese investment would grow enormously.[138]

Already the leaders of Poland and Hungary are lauding what the Chinese are doing. The Polish authorities describe

the 16+1 as a 'tremendous opportunity'. In Budapest, it is referred to as the 'Eastern Opening'. But what is clear is that for
the Chinese the 16+1 is about both commercial and strategic
interests. It is about taking the commercial opportunities that
exist in eastern Europe, yes, but also about China's Belt and
Road Initiative, which the *Financial Times* has described as
an attempt to 'win both markets and diplomatic allies in the
sixty-four countries between Asia and Europe'.[139] And the way
in which the 16+1 is run and managed also tells a story. The
secretariat is based in Beijing and run by the Chinese Foreign
Ministry. Although multilateral in appearance, China uses it
as a framework within which to pursue one-sided bilateral
relations with individual eastern European states. In a post-
EU Europe, those relationships would become even more
one-sided. And as with Trump, so with the Chinese leader, Xi
Jinping: the price for inward Chinese investment is likely to
be compliance with some of China's wishes and support for
some of China's aims on the wider international stage. And
if the experience of Chinese investment in Africa is anything
to go by, the one thing China will not demand in return for
its investment is a commitment to any kind of democracy or
respect for human rights. In fact, with the EU gone, and with
both China and Russia seeking to advance their interests in
the eastern and south-eastern parts of Europe, the autocratic
forces at work to undermine democracy in that part of the
continent would be large and difficult to stop.

The inescapable conclusion, in structural terms, is that the balance of power in Europe after the European Union will once again be multipolar. Some of the actors may be different to those in earlier periods of Europe's history, but many will be the same. The challenge for all will be how to manage such a balance of power in a peaceful and responsible way, given the many risks and challenges attendant upon its resurrection.

THE THREAT TO PEACE

The prevalent attitude to these risks among many in the west of Europe appears to be to ridicule and dismiss them. David Cameron was given a dose of this treatment during the Brexit referendum campaign when he talked, albeit briefly, about the dangers to Europe's security if the EU unravelled. But underpinning the derision is a belief which itself is unsustainable, namely that not only has Europe managed to buy a ticket out of its violent past, but that the journey is inevitably and only one way. War does indeed seem a very remote possibility for those living in the geopolitically sheltered western part of Europe. But those who live in central and eastern Europe, the Balkans and the Caucasus are far less sanguine. This is not only because they experienced the sharper end of the fighting during the Second World War but because in recent years war has been a reality in places like Croatia, Bosnia-Herzegovina, Georgia and Ukraine.

The same people in the West who dismiss concerns for peace tend also to be the ones who frame Europe's central challenge as a defence of the status quo against many threats. This too is wrong-headed. As a perspective, it does not capture what has already been happening in post-Cold War Europe, nor does it provide a standpoint that would be useful in a post-EU world. If the EU collapses the status quo will have ceased to exist. A massive wave of change will be unleashed. In truth, though, this will only add to a process of change that has already started and is almost constant. Since the end of the Cold War alone we have seen the re-unification of Germany and the dissolution of Yugoslavia, Czechoslovakia and the Soviet Union. We have seen the birth of some new European states and the rebirth of others. And to that mix must now be added the many secessionist movements that are gaining a measure of traction across the continent, from Scotland to Catalonia. These movements remain committed, by definition, to more changes to the European map. The challenge today therefore, and the challenge in any post-EU scenario, is not best thought of as a status quo to be defended but as a process of change that needs to be managed. It is a challenge that will have to be faced in the context of a continent divided and in which Russia especially is newly emboldened.

We saw in Chapter 1 how Russia seeks to win friends and influence people. If it can use intimidating military exercises, cyber-attacks, fake news campaigns, and networks of bribery and corruption inside the EU even while the EU and NATO still exist, one can easily imagine what it might get up to with the EU and NATO removed from the scene. A more aggressive approach to Ukraine should be anticipated, up to and including the deployment of regular Russian forces on Ukrainian territory. Russia would almost certainly also try to instigate a form of regime change in Kiev to get a government in place there that was more in alignment with the views of the Kremlin. Belarus would also stand little chance of defining its own path. It is already closely linked to Russia both culturally and through a number of economic integration and military agreements. It was a founding member of the Russian-led customs union that eventually became the Eurasian Economic Union and is a member of the Collective Security Treaty Organisation. Its membership of the latter has facilitated Russian efforts to incorporate Belarusian territory into the Russian air defence network, and Russian and Belarusian military forces regularly exercise together. But the authorities in Minsk have tried from time to time to assert their independence, being reticent about recognising the Russian annexation of Crimea and seeking to balance their ties to Russia with more outreach to the West. With the European Union gone, and NATO either gone with it or not credible, Russia would perceive little obstacle to doing whatever was necessary to ensure that Belarus too was firmly in its orbit.

In a post-EU and effectively post-NATO scenario, all three Baltic states of Latvia, Lithuania and Estonia would also be in an extremely exposed position. They would be subject to Russian military intimidation and to attempts at penetration and destabilisation, perhaps up to the point where claimed mistreatment of some Russian minorities in the Baltic states was used as a pretext for military intervention. Poland would be a much more difficult challenge for the Russians, but it too would be subject to intimidation, extensive cyber-attack and disinformation campaigns. Poland's former foreign minister Radosław Sikorski once expressed a desire for Poland to be a player in European politics. More likely in a post-EU Europe is that he would find it had reverted to its former role as a playing field. Finland has traversed the path to a stable relationship with Russia very skilfully for a number of decades now and may fare better. But if a Nordic bloc of countries took on deeper and more meaningful defence dimensions, it could meet with forceful Russian disapproval. Further south, Georgia would be a vassal state, as would Moldova. A major Russian effort to capture a Bulgarian state and economy that it has already done much to penetrate would seem obvious. And across the Balkans, in places like Serbia, Montenegro and Greece, Russia would use a combination of pan-Slavic identity or the ties of the Orthodox Church alongside financial and other instruments in the pursuit of increased influence.

The Russians would not have it all their own way and in terms of the peace and stability of the whole of post-EU Europe, therein lies the danger. The new Chinese role in central and eastern Europe would be a complicating factor for the Kremlin, and unless something dramatic happens to halt China's economic progress, Beijing would have far deeper pockets than Moscow. Europe could become a point of tension in their own bilateral relationship. In some parts of Europe, such as in the Balkans, things would likely get very messy in a more general sense, with a potential four-way contest for markets and diplomatic influence involving Russia, Turkey, China and Germany.

Perhaps the central question of post-EU European politics, in fact, concerns the attitude to Russia to be taken by Germany. Berlin would have to confront anew the question of whether it wanted to be the capital of a European Germany, committed to the values enshrined in Article 2 of the Lisbon Treaty, even after the EU itself had ceased to exist, or whether it was a capital pursuing a German Europe, acting more in its own more narrowly defined self-interest, even if that sometimes came at the expense of the smaller states of the continent.[140]

If it chose the former option, that would probably set it on a collision course with Russia, and see it acting in defence of the remnants of a Europe of rules and laws against a Russian approach dominated by power politics. If it did choose to go this way, however, the German leadership would have to decide how much of eastern and south-eastern Europe to contest with Russia in economic and political terms. It would need to ask how much support it was willing to give to the Baltic states, Poland and others as part of that struggle. And it would need to seek, and find, others in Europe and outside it who were willing to help it in that endeavour. Most controversially, it would need to think about a significant increase in German defence spending and, given that Russia has nuclear weapons and Germany does not, to give serious consideration to the development or acquisition by other means of a German nuclear deterrent.

Choosing the alternative course, of accepting that Europe was now a zone of competitive power politics in which Germany had to play by power politics rules, might also seem at first to imply German competition with Russia. Over time, however, it could lead to the implicit and pragmatic acceptance of agreed spheres of influence between them. Concerns have already been raised about Germany's willingness to go over the heads of the eastern Europeans to do deals with Russia, especially with regard to gas pipeline construction. But these concerns are overdone. The notion of accepting spheres of influence and of nakedly subordinating the interests of some of the smaller states in Europe remains anathema to many in the Germany of today. In a post-EU Europe, however, there are two reasons for pessimism with regard to whether they could be avoided. The first is that it is hard to see Russian behaviour changing, and the second is that the risks of open confrontation with Russia may be deemed just too high by the German leadership.

NEW SPHERES OF INFLUENCE?

Contrary to much Western commentary about it being driven entirely by the personality of Vladimir Putin, Russian behaviour is in fact shaped by a deep-rooted world view. It is a view accepted as legitimate by much of the Russian elite and it dominates the thinking of pretty much the entire national security and foreign policy establishment in Moscow. This view stresses the extent to which the post-Cold War order in Europe has been built according to a Western design, a design that chose to bypass President Gorbachev's talk of 'conflict transcendence' and to replace it with the gradual expansion eastwards of NATO and the EU. In this account, Russia's legitimate security interests as a great power, recognised (as those of the Soviet Union) at the Yalta and Potsdam conferences of 1945, have been consistently relegated or ignored. Western institutions, moreover, have become more anti-Russian as they have taken on board such sentiments as expressed by their newer eastern European members. A growing number of military and national security officials in Moscow now also appear to believe that the West is determined not only to overthrow President Putin but to weaken

Russia to the point where it might be effectively destroyed and dismembered. There is deep suspicion of Western involvement in the countries neighbouring Russia as a result and also a fear of encirclement by the US and its allies. The Russian narrative on what has happened in Ukraine, namely that the democratically elected Yanukovych government was overthrown by a Western- and primarily US-backed unconstitutional coup, is a part of this mindset. Even the Russian narrative on sovereignty is different to the one prevailing in the West.[141] For many in the latter, the utility of the traditional notion of sovereignty has become questionable at best in recent years. It is seen as being eroded by notions such as an international responsibility to protect civilians in other states on the one hand and by the effects of globalisation and higher levels of interdependence on the other. In the pre-Trump era, the West sought to grapple with this and even embrace it as a new reality suggestive of the need to pursue much greater levels of multilateral cooperation. Russia, however, sees the Western narrative on 21st-century sovereignty as a mere cover for intervention in the affairs of other states in the West's own interests. In the Russian view, it is the failure by the West to accept more traditional notions of sovereignty that sows distrust, makes international cooperation more difficult, and means a disordered world is more likely.[142]

The Russian position on this is deeply hypocritical, since as a state it so obviously disregards the claims to sovereignty of its own neighbours. And there are many in the West who are totally dismissive of its entire account of post-Cold War European politics as a fantasy dreamt up merely to justify Putin's aggression. I have also lost count of the number of times I have been regaled by east European and Baltic leadership figures with stories of offers of cooperation made to Moscow and rebuffed. Some of this criticism is justified, some not. What seems clear to me, and what would need to matter most from the point of view of policymakers in Berlin and other European capitals in the post-EU scenario being contemplated here, is that it is the world view that shapes Russian behaviour.

In Russian eyes, Russia is a great power that has been disrespected. While members of the EU have congratulated themselves on achieving a higher state of being, and of slipping the leash of a world characterised by power politics in particular, the perception of the Russian elite is that power politics never left Europe and that Russia has been at the wrong end of it, having suffered a prolonged period of weakness. With what it now sees as its power restored, it is ready to claim the rights that it believes great powers have. Those rights include control of other states in one's neighbourhood when the national interest demands it. Nor is there comfort to be had in thinking this is a temporary Russian position that will not outlast Putin. It is a view that predates him, and will most likely long survive him. In its interpretation of post-Cold War events it was already on show as far back as 1991 in the dispute over Western military intervention in Yugoslavia.[143] In many respects it is rooted in Russian foreign policy thinking that predates even the Soviet Union. It is noticed more in Putin's time, because he has stabilised and recovered Russia's position to the point where its views can no longer be disregarded.

The point is that Russia and its way of thinking about European and international affairs is a reality that has to be reckoned with. In a situation in which the EU has collapsed and NATO with it, not only will Russia perceive a major strategic opportunity to extend its influence and footprint across the continent, but almost its entire elite will tell itself it is fully justified in doing so. Any state attempting to confront this Russian approach and the mentality that underpins it will be taking huge risks. It will have to do this in a context in which most if not all of the conflict prevention and crisis management arrangements built in an earlier period of great power confrontation in Europe have been allowed to atrophy or disappear. The task will require a willingness not only to engage in sub-military competition but, ultimately, to contemplate war. Berlin, in my view, will be unlikely to take it on alone and in a divided and acrimonious continent, and with the US focused elsewhere, it is highly uncertain as to whether a wider coalition could be assembled to do so. Having thought things through, it is my guess that the German leadership will pragmatically adopt a policy of accommodation of some Russian interests and that Berlin will seek to prioritise its own relationship with Russia over and above the interests of those in eastern Europe who may wish otherwise.

AN UNSTABLE CONTINENT

Even that path will bring its dangers, because in many respects Europe after the European Union will be a more dangerous place than it was during the Cold War. Then, the continent was divided and had far more nuclear weapons on its territory than it does today, including many on a high state of alert. The situation was fraught and few would wish to go back to it. But a military balance of sorts was preserved, underpinned not only by nuclear deterrence but eventually by arms control agreements too. Spheres of influence existed and for the most part both sides recognised them and acted accordingly. Over time, and especially after the close encounter with Armageddon represented by the Cuban Missile Crisis in 1962, crisis prevention and crisis management procedures were put in place to limit the risks. Intense espionage, hot conflict by proxy in other parts of the world, and a variety of sub-military forms of competition continued, but the Cold War stayed cold. By its end, its protagonists had managed to transition it from unmanaged competition to managed stand-off.[144]

In Europe after the EU the challenge will have to be faced all over again. Even without a fundamental confrontation of political ideas between the major powers it will be hard to avoid conflict. The challenge will not be to manage a status quo in the context of recognised spheres of influence and an agreed set of rules, but to manage an unfolding process of historical change on a continent whose rules have just imploded, where no recognised spheres of influence exist, and in a landscape littered with potential points of great-power friction. There is no reason to suppose that the political class and leadership elite that had failed to keep the EU together in the first place can find the wisdom and statecraft to rise to that challenge. And there is no reason either to suppose, where that elite has been replaced by one more nationalist in tone and policy content, that the outcome will be any better. If anything, it will be worse.

History seems to teach us that the successful management of a balance of power can be achieved for a time but not indefinitely.[145] It is a feat sometimes achieved by earlier generations of Europeans and on occasion, even for a prolonged period, but it is also one that in the end, and quite spectacularly, they were unable to sustain. A post-EU Europe will be inherently unstable. We may see wars in eastern Europe that trigger refugee flows to the west on a similar scale to those recently experienced from the south. We may see smaller wars into which larger European powers are pulled or miscalculations of interest that trigger conflict between them. And we may once again see a Europe where smaller states have their interests totally disregarded by those with greater clout. What we are unlikely to see, for a very long time at least, is a Europe of cooperative institutions and behaviours underpinned by common values and some shared rules of the road. We would not necessarily experience the new Dark Age that Winston Churchill warned of in 1940, but if the EU collapses we will be much nearer to it than to the sunlit uplands for which he and so many other Europeans fought.[146]

PART 3

AVOIDING THE WORST

CHAPTER 10

WHAT IS TO BE DONE?

I finish this book where I began, by reaffirming that it should be seen as a warning rather than as a prediction. One does not issue warnings unless one thinks they are necessary and throughout the course of preceding chapters I have tried to establish four propositions that collectively demonstrate why this one should be heeded.

The first is that the European Union remains today in a deep state of crisis, sustained there by a mix of external threats and internal weaknesses more profound than at any other time in its history. The external threats come not only from the east, but for the first time since the EU's creation from both the south and the west too. Vladimir Putin, Donald Trump and Bashar al-Assad are very different political figures whose methods of wielding power vary enormously but from the perspective of the EU, they combine to represent a sea of trouble. Internally, the euro crisis may be in abeyance but fundamentally it has still not been resolved.

The commitment of a eurozone elite, spanning both left and right politically, to a prolonged period of austerity as part of the answer to the crisis has fuelled the argument that all of the established political forces in Europe are the same, while what unites them is their desire to run a system that is rigged against 'the people'. The damage done by the crisis has helped propel an anti-establishment mood that may yet fuel a breakthrough for Eurosceptic nationalism in one or more major EU member states. The decision at the height of the euro crisis to sanctify private debt and not to countenance a far bigger role for sovereign and bank debt restructuring has also had profound consequences. It is an approach that took a problem between creditors and debtors and turned it into one between nations and states, doing much to damage solidarity between EU member states in the process.

The Brexit referendum in the UK also illustrated not only the particularities of this country's relationship with Europe but the ways in which the EU's own weaknesses could be used against it by the political forces wishing to do it harm. The euro crisis was used very effectively to underpin the argument that the UK was better off out of the EU, not only better off out of the euro. The severe downturn in the European economy increased the flow of migrants to Britain at a time when immigration concerns were already rising, serving as grist to the mill of those who wanted immigration to be *the* issue. The chaos and division with which the EU attempted to manage the migrant and refugee crisis in the south was also exploited ruthlessly by UKIP and others to show that the EU was both hopeless and incompetent.

Second, I have argued that while the EU and several of its leaders have engaged in serious efforts at reform to address the different dimensions of the crisis, those reforms have so far not been enough. I have tried to be fair in arriving at that assessment. I do not dismiss lightly the effort and expenditure of political capital that has been involved in getting this far. The various measures to address the flaws in the architecture of the single currency, including steps towards both a banking and a capital markets union, and the creation of the Fiscal Compact, have a claim to the mantle of progress. In some respects, the sanctions imposed on Russia over Ukraine and the diplomatic steps taken to help stem the flow of migrants and refugees from Europe's south have also been impressive, though so far, the latter has been far more effective than the former in changing actual behaviour on the ground. On defence and security, measures like the creation of a border force and the European Commission's first foray into investment in defence research and development are new and worthwhile advances stimulated by recent events.

And yet. One often gets the sense that everyone in Brussels wants credit for making progress against where things were yesterday, as though that were the really important measure of success. Often absent is the sense that there is an objective reality outside the Brussels bubble that may demand assessment against different, more fundamental criteria. The problem is that it is a question of when, not if, that reality bites. The doom loop between Europe's governments and their banks has not been broken, a reality that will be brutally exposed if a new crisis comes. The gaps in the regulation of the financial system give no confidence that a further financial crisis can avoided. The Fiscal Compact and even more the new drive for a fiscal union, at President Macron's instigation, may feed the politics of division between member states rather than foster the solidarity they are supposed to demonstrate. The sanctions against Russia have not worked. On migration the EU is dangerously reliant on the rapidly emergent Turkish autocracy of President Erdoğan. And on defence, words still fill the gap where serious, strategically significant collaboration ought to be. Politics may indeed be the art of the possible. The worry must be that future events will show the possible has just not been enough.

This judgement underpins the third proposition advanced by the book, namely that if more is not done to address the threats facing the European Union and to overcome its remaining weaknesses, it will remain vulnerable to a wide range of events that could trigger its collapse. I presented six such trigger events but could have added more. The length of the possible list of triggers that seem plausible and that could ultimately be devastating for the European Union itself tells a story. Only some of what could go wrong needs to for the EU to be pushed to, and possibly over, the edge. For the EU to survive, everything has to go right. What, one might legitimately ask, are the chances of that?

Which leads to the necessity of considering what the consequences might be if the worst does happen. The final proposition I have advanced is that the collapse of the EU would be an unmitigated disaster with the potential to drive Europeans into economic, political and geopolitical confrontation with one another. This is an admittedly dystopian analysis but I believe it has to be taken seriously. In the wake of an EU collapse there would be many who would be motivated to try to salvage the best of what it had to offer. My case is not that those people, and the sentiment that they would embody, would be few in number and without relevance. It is that the structural conditions in which post-EU Europe was operating would be heavily stacked against them. The dynamics of economic disintegration and recession, and of the necessity for simple explanations of what has gone wrong, strongly suggest an era of blame-game politics where those responsible for the bad times are other Europeans. Political expediency would be likely to drive the tactical adoption of such a stance even among those politicians less inclined to be true believers. There is no telling, as the last chapter made clear, where that might end.

DEFINING THE NECESSARY:
A BATTLE ON FIVE FRONTS

A lively debate is under way among observers and commentators with regard to what needs to happen next. There are suggestions for the EU to pursue some populist policies of its own. These could centre on doing far more to tackle corporate tax avoidance; action to address corruption in countries where it is endemic and where helping to do something about it would help to make the EU popular; and taking steps to give a boost to Europe's green economy, to appeal to the young. The issue of moving to a more multi-speed Europe is also back on the agenda in a big way, in the hope of providing the flexibility required for states to be members of the EU while preserving a variety of different forms of relationship with it. Some even see this as a way for the UK to maintain a form of membership of the EU in the longer run, as part of an outer circle of countries surrounding a more integrated core.

There is space for each of these ideas and all could contribute something positive. They should be pursued for the simple reason that they are each the right thing to do, and not only because they hold out a prospect of helping the EU out of its current predicament. But if the EU is to survive it seems to me that the real action, in the shorter term at least, is going to have to be somewhere else. It is crucial that additional measures are taken to address five aspects of the crisis in particular.

Addressing Migration at Source

On the migration challenge, the EU is not going to come to an internal consensus on welcoming and distributing large numbers of migrants in the near future. The answer will have to be found elsewhere. It would help with the politics of the issue, as well as with the reality, if further measures to strengthen the external borders of the EU were introduced. The EU also needs to raise its game with regard to joining up databases to allow law enforcement a better chance of identifying and catching both criminals and terrorists as they enter the Union. And agreeing a better stance on refugees, as opposed to economic migrants, is both a moral and a legal necessity. A smoother process for resettling refugees with a real and legitimate claim to be in the EU must be established and a better process for facilitating the return home of those denied asylum must be its accompaniment. These measures will do nothing to alter the underlying drivers of the migration and refugee surge, however, nor to reduce reliance on Turkey, so the EU must also look well beyond its own shores and borders to address migration at source. This means a large increase in aid provided to sub-Saharan Africa, into the countries from which many economic migrants come. This will be needed not only to help provide economic alternatives to those who will otherwise make the journey to Europe, but also to alter the balance of incentives for governments in the region so as to encourage them to assist the EU in its endeavour. Remittances from migrant workers in Europe are an important revenue source for many countries and a replacement funding source for that will also be required. The EU will have to provide it. It will also need to step up its conflict prevention efforts in the southern neighbourhood, since conflict is one of the major drivers of current flows to Europe. There was a time when such policies were considered by some to be a liberal nicety. Today, if the EU is to survive by taking the heat out of the migrant and refugee debate inside the Union, they must be seen as a strategic necessity.

Breaking the Bank–Government Doom Loop

A second area where further change is vital relates to the doom loop between governments and banks. Either the doom loop exists or it is broken. At the time of writing and despite EU reforms put in place up to the early part of 2018, it still exists. If allowed to persist, there is a very good chance that the next financial or economic crisis to hit the EU will kill it. The Banking Union must therefore be completed. Rules to resolve failing banks via bail-ins rather than taxpayer-funded bail-outs must be applied rigorously and consistently across the eurozone. There must also be a big reduction in the extent to which banks are allowed to hold concentrations of bonds issued by their own governments. These two steps would make it much harder for a banking crisis to create a sovereign debt crisis on the one hand, and for a sovereign debt crisis to trigger a banking crisis on the other. In addition, there needs to be a large increase in the Single Resolution Fund such that when bank resolutions are necessary, a larger common European fund is available to help recapitalise them.

Pursuing Fiscal Decentralisation

Third, a new way of managing eurozone fiscal policy needs to be found. At the moment, the debate seems to suggest the establishment of a fiscal union. As discussed earlier in this book, President Macron has called for one. The German Chancellor will probably agree, though in watered-down form. Others are arguing to go even further with the creation of a full fiscal *and* political union, involving not only a common eurozone budget and significant fiscal transfers to the EU's poorer regions, but also the issuance of some common eurozone debt in the form of Eurobonds. In this model, eurozone member states would effectively share sovereignty over fiscal policy. Whether in the Macron formulation or in this more ambitious version, the suggestion is that a common authority is needed to oversee things, either in the form of a eurozone finance minister or a eurozone government.

While this direction of travel might make economic sense to some, it seems to me that it would be politically disastrous. It would double-down on the approach that has destroyed much solidarity between member states by putting in lights the fact that membership of the single currency requires fiscal transfers from the wealthier to the poorer regions on an ongoing basis. This already happens through EU structural funds but a fiscal union would change the politics of these transfers, would increase them in scale, and could destroy support for the single currency in a country like Germany as a result. At the same time, maintaining the rules embodied in the current Fiscal Compact on both budget deficits and overall debt levels is likely to be the price of German engagement. This will reinforce the sense that single currency membership means national governments have little room for manoeuvre on fiscal policy. It will leave national democratic deliberations and choices, in a country like Greece for example, largely devoid of content, and it is this dynamic that has already allowed Eurosceptic populists to argue that all mainstream politicians supporting the euro are the same. There is some truth to their argument. Imposing a fiscal straitjacket on eurozone member states has had the effect of shackling mainstream political debate and has left the populists looking like they are the only ones offering an alternative.

Instead of pursuing a fiscal union, it would be far better for the future of the eurozone and therefore of the European Union if an agreement was reached to decentralise fiscal policy and make clear that it was a national responsibility.

To ensure this produced a sound fiscal stance overall, such an agreement should contain a commitment by all eurozone member states to pursue strongly counter-cyclical policies. That is to say, in recessions they should be allowed and indeed expected to spend more to help counter the downturn, provided that in the good times they rein in spending to prevent constant accumulations of debt. This would not only make sense economically but would expand the space for disagreement and difference among mainstream political parties on questions of national economic strategy and squeeze the economic policy space the populists have grown used to occupying without challenge as a result. It would also make it far harder for the Eurosceptics to argue that national governments were economically powerless by virtue of single currency membership. It would be a flexible system where the current Fiscal Compact lacks flexibility and it would be an approach to eurozone management embedded in a pro-EU political strategy. At the moment the debate tends to resemble an economic one with a bit of politics thrown in as an afterthought.

It is advisable too, in relation to this debate, to keep in mind the diversity of reasons that led countries into trouble in the last eurozone crisis. The myth that that crisis was primarily caused by fiscal imprudence should not be allowed to persist or to excessively shape the policy response. Ireland, for example, was not Greece. For most of the countries caught up in the last crisis, the cause was not that their public finances had been so badly mismanaged as to make them unsustainable, but that the decision to respond to the global financial crisis with taxpayer bail-outs of failing banks resulted in much higher levels of public debt. With the Banking Union's provisions for bail-ins rather than bail-outs in place and fully operational in future, it would be harder for this to happen again. The disastrous mismanagement and corruption of the public finances in some countries, of the kind that *was* experienced in Greece prior to 2009, does have to be guarded against, and this should be done with new eurozone-wide measures on monitoring, transparency and anti-corruption rather than through inflexible limits on public spending whatever the economic circumstances. But eurozone fiscal policy does not need to be run as though every country outside Germany is inflicted with an incurable case of fiscal incontinence.

Nor should returning fiscal policy to the national level require the declaration of a 'no bail-out' rule for eurozone governments. Although some, especially in Germany, might want such a rule to make clear that the costs of any future sovereign default would be borne only by the country concerned, the introduction of a no-bail-out rule for governments would have two potentially very negative effects. It could help undermine some governments with larger debts and precipitate a crisis where there currently is none or, alternatively, it could persuade governments fearing a crisis to pursue excessive and self-defeating fiscal contractions that, far from shoring up their position against a future crisis, would actually be more likely to trigger one by damaging demand and growth. In my view, even in a system where fiscal policy is clearly a national responsibility, proposals to convert the current European Stability Mechanism (ESM) into a European Monetary Fund (EMF) would still make sense and have an important and positive role to play. As a bail-out fund of last resort for eurozone governments, the EMF would help provide confidence in eurozone governments and in the event that a country had to turn to it, loans would still be subject to the kinds of conditions currently associated with the ESM. Those who argue that this kind of European support is only politically viable in creditor countries if those likely to ask for help have taken on the binding and rigid commitments embodied in the Fiscal Compact or something like it must be challenged. In the name of providing a stability mechanism they understand is vital to protecting the single currency economically, they are trying to lock in a commitment to such economic inflexibility that they are very likely to create the conditions that would destroy it politically.

Dealing with Trump and Putin

Fourth, the European Union needs a strategy to survive Donald Trump and one to defend itself against Vladimir

Putin. With regard to Trump, the occasional protest against his words and actions will not suffice. A more systematic response is essential and this will need a number of tracks to be run in parallel. Support should be given to Trump where this is not objectionable, for example on tackling some unfair Chinese trade practices. So long as this is done within the framework of World Trade Organization rules and not via unilateral actions and megaphone diplomacy, this is sensible. But attempts to change Trump's mind in other areas should also be actively and creatively pursued. One opportunity might be to help the military leaders he now listens to make the case that climate change will be deeply damaging to US security interests around the world. If he won't buy the argument on environmental grounds, perhaps he can be persuaded to change stance on security grounds instead.

Elsewhere, alternatives to his approaches will need to be offered, especially where his current policy is dangerous. More active European diplomacy will almost certainly be needed in the Middle East in the EU's own defence. The nuclear deal with Iran will need to be defended by the Europeans who helped negotiate it. Action on better regulation of global finance ought to be high up the list, as opposed to Trump's policy of deregulating Wall Street, and the very idea that multilateral cooperation and a rules-based order is a good thing, one that the EU actually after all embodies, must be argued for and defended. Ultimately, the EU collectively and European states individually will need to think through how to insure against the worst damage Trump could do.

Nowhere is this more important than on the issue of defence. Nothing should be done from the European side to undermine NATO, but nor is total reliance on NATO for security any longer the no-brainer that it once was. Europeans must take more responsibility for their own defence. Moving forward, the EU countries should pursue the maximum amount of defence cooperation they can achieve, but for all the reasons set out earlier in the book I remain sceptical as to how far this can and will go in practice. So every effort should also be made to ensure Brexit does not undermine Europe's defence capability and one of the main goals of Brexit negotiations should be to make sure close cooperation between the two sides continues after the UK has left. And alongside EU-wide efforts, bilateral UK–French cooperation should be deepened. There is no viable approach to European strategic autonomy that would not be built on a UK–French platform. These two nuclear-armed European states with permanent seats on the UN Security Council are Europe's major defence and diplomatic assets – all the more so in the age of Trump.

With regard to Putin, sanctions should be maintained on Russia indefinitely given the lack of progress in Ukraine. They may be largely ineffective in delivering their primary objective of changes to Russian behaviour but they remain of symbolic importance. While the EU and NATO should avoid any impression that they intend to contest Russian influence by force in places like Ukraine, the EU does have an interest in being adjacent to neighbours in the east that share its values and want to cooperate closely with it. Because of that, the EU should strengthen its non-military support to countries in the region and revamp its policy towards the entire eastern neighbourhood.

More also can and should be done to tackle Russian activity aimed at destabilising the EU. This will require a major expansion of the current effort to counter Russian disinformation campaigns. Even more important perhaps is to understand and counter the underlying Russian strategy. In many respects the Russians understand the politics and economics of EU member states better than those states do themselves. They try to identify flaws, fissures and perceived injustices in EU societies and to seek to exploit them to sow division. Where the EU and its member states fail to ensure sufficient transparency in the financial system or due process in public procurement processes, for example, the Russians see an opportunity to launder funds, buy influence and win major contracts using questionable means. EU state capture can be the end result. Where a population inside the EU is less well off than some others, such as the Russian-speaking population in rural parts of Latvia, the Russians seek to make something of it. Where a state mismanages a nationalist and secessionist challenge, as the Spanish government has done in relation to Catalonia, Russia sees a chance to spread disinformation to try to maximise the damage. The response to this has to be for Europeans inside the EU to get their own house in order. The commitment to well-governed, law-based, democratic systems that treat their citizens equally and fairly not just in legal terms but in economic ones as well is vital. The commitment not to resist legitimate aspirations for change, and to address all political challenges through dialogue, not repression, is also crucial. It not only reflects who and what the EU is supposed to represent but reduces the space for Russian subterfuge and limits the reach of the lies it tries to peddle.

A Europe to Inspire Loyalty

Lastly, the European Union must fight more forcefully for the values that it is supposed to embody. As noted in Chapter 8, the EU Commission concluded in 2016 that Poland's government was threatening the independence of the courts and the rule of law. The European Parliament expressed a similar view. It was right that in December 2017 the Commission went further with a recommendation that Article 7 of the Treaty on European Union be invoked against Poland in an attempt to stop the drift to authoritarianism there. Effective action may be difficult to secure in the end but it is important that it be attempted for two reasons.

First, the EU's ability to persuade aspirant members in eastern and south-eastern Europe to take a commitment to democratic values seriously is on the line. At the moment, the attraction of EU membership can still be influential in spreading these values to parts of Europe where they are not well established. A failure to fight for them inside the EU could have a very negative effect. In fact, there is a danger that a combination of EU weakness on this point with growing Russian and Chinese influence could, over time, be deadly to the democratic prospects of the region.

Second, a commitment to the rule of law, democracy and human rights is what makes the EU stand out from many other parts of the world. This not only needs to serve as a pole of attraction for those outside the Union but as a source of inspiration for those already living in it. Where President Macron *was* right in 2017 was in declaring that it was time to fight for the idea of Europe. To do that, we have to be clear about what that idea is. We also have to acknowledge that this is not the time to defend Europe in primarily institutional or procedural terms but in ideological ones. Fundamentally Europe means a commitment to liberal values, to individual freedom, to equality and to cooperation among nations in the belief that we, as Europeans, can achieve more together than we can alone. If that idea of Europe is made clear and reflected in action, the EU still has a chance to command the support and loyalty of many of its citizens and to mobilise them to defend it. It can use these founding values as the high bar against which to assess today's imperfect Union, and as the basis for a call to citizens and civil society groups alike to help make it better. If it fails to do that, the EU itself will surely fail too.

In the introduction to this book, I said it was hard to feel optimistic. Part of the reason for that is that none of the measures I have outlined in this chapter can be implemented easily. Getting the Germans on board with fiscal decentralisation would be challenging to say the least. Persuading the Italian government to face up to the challenge of what bail-ins of its failing banks would mean for the savings of its own citizens would be just as hard. A big expansion of overseas aid to help address migration at source would be a tough sell for many who think, and argue, that Europe's money should be spent at home. The prospects of really getting influence on Trump, and of agreeing new approaches to deal with Putin, are highly uncertain. And whatever the Commission tries to do to address growing authoritarianism inside the EU, countries like Hungary and Poland are likely to support each other to ensure effective action is vetoed.

Much of the governing elite in Europe today is desperately hoping that what seems possible politically will prove to be enough to save the EU. But what the moment actually requires is a set of politicians who can make the reforms that are necessary politically possible. We must hope such politicians can be found. If they are not, the EU will at some point collapse and we will all be living in Europe after the European Union. Nothing less than the seven decades of peace, relative prosperity and progress that the EU represents is now on the line and everyone alive in Europe today, and many outside it, will be negatively affected if the EU disintegrates and passes into history. One can hope it will go on to thrive and prosper and the suggestions I have made here would help move it in that direction. As we move towards the end of the second decade of the century, however, hope seems a very long way from expectation.

SELECT BIBLIOGRAPHY

Allison, Roy, *Russia, the West, and Military Intervention* (Oxford: Oxford University Press, 2013).

Ash, Timothy Garton, *In Europe's Name: Germany and the Divided Continent* (London: Vintage, 1994).

Blyth, Mark, *Austerity: The History of a Dangerous Idea* (Oxford: Oxford University Press, 2013).

Byrne, Liam, *Black Flag Down: Counter-Extremism, Defeating ISIS and Winning the Battle of Ideas* (London: Biteback, 2016).

Djankov, Simeon, *Inside the Euro Crisis: An Eyewitness Account* (Washington, DC: Peterson Institute for International Economics, 2014).

The European Crisis and its Human Cost: A Call for Fair Alternatives and Solutions, Caritas Monitoring Report, 2014.

Ford, Robert and Goodwin, Matthew, *Revolt on the Right: Explaining Support for the Radical Right in Britain* (Abingdon: Routledge, 2014).

Gaddis, John Lewis, *The Cold War: The Deals, The Spies, The Lies, The Truth* (London: Penguin, 2007).

Goodhart, David, *The Road to Somewhere: The Populist Revolt and the Future of Politics* (London: Hurst, 2017).

Graham, David A., 'The Mysterious Life and Death of Abdelhamid Abaaoud', *The Atlantic*, 19 November 2015.

Hewitt, Gavin, *The Lost Continent: Europe's Darkest Hour since World War Two* (London: Hodder & Stoughton, 2013).

Hoffman, David E., *The Dead Hand: Reagan, Gorbachev and the Untold Story of the Cold War Arms Race* (London: Icon, 2011).

Judt, Tony, *Postwar: A History of Europe Since 1945* (London: Vintage, 2010).

Kearns, Ian and Murray, Kate, *The Age of Trump* (London: Fabian Society, 2017).

Krastev, Ivan, *After Europe* (Philadelphia: University of Pennsylvania Press, 2017).

Legrain, Philippe, *European Spring: Why Our Economies and Politics Are in a Mess – And How to Put Them Right* (Charleston, SC: CB Creative Books, 2014).

Leonard, Mark, *Why Europe Will Run the 21st Century* (London: Fourth Estate, 2005).

Luce, Edward, *The Retreat of Western Liberalism* (London: Little, Brown, 2017).

MacShane, Denis, *Brexit: How Britain Left Europe* (London: I. B. Tauris, 2016).

Müller, Jan-Werner, *What Is Populism?* (London: Penguin, 2017).

Owen, David, *Europe Restructured? The Eurozone Crisis and its Aftermath* (York: Methuen, 2012).

Pisani-Ferry, Jean, *The Euro-Crisis and Its Aftermath* (Oxford: Oxford University Press, 2011).

Richards, Steve, *The Rise of the Outsiders: How Mainstream Politics Lost Its Way* (London: Atlantic, 2017).

Sandbu, Martin, *Europe's Orphan: The Future of the Euro and the Politics of Debt* (Princeton: Princeton University Press, 2015).

Shipman, Tim, *All Out War: The Full Story of How Brexit Sank Britain's Political Class* (London: William Collins, 2016).

Stiglitz, Joseph E., *The Euro: How a Common Currency Threatens the Future of Europe* (New York: W. W. Norton, 2016).

Stokes, Bruce, 'The Immigration Crisis is Tearing Europe Apart', *Foreign Policy*, 22 July 2016.

Streek, Wolfgang, *Buying Time: The Delayed Crisis of Democratic Capitalism* (London: Verso, 2017).

Taylor, A. J. P., *The Struggle for Mastery in Europe 1848–1918* (Oxford: Oxford University Press, 1954).

Varoufakis, Yanis, *And the Weak Suffer What They Must? Europe, Austerity and the Threat to Global Stability* (London: Vintage, 2016).

Zielonka, Jan, *Is the EU Doomed?* (London: Polity, 2014).

NOTES

Chapter 1: Europe under Siege

1. For a rounded take on what Trump means for Europe, drawing on thinkers from both Europe and the US, see Ian Kearns and Kate Murray, *The Age of Trump* (London: Fabian Society, 2017).

2. Lizzie Dearden, 'Russian cyber attacks have targeted UK energy, communication and media networks, says top security chief', *The Independent*, 15 November 2017.

3. Mark Scott and Diego Torres, 'Catalan referendum stokes fears of Russian influence', *Politico*, Europe edition, 30 September 2017.

4. Heather A. Conley et al., *The Kremlin Playbook: Understanding Russian Influence in Central and Eastern Europe* (Washington: Center for Strategic and International Studies, 2016).

5. Fredrik Wesslau, 'Putin's friends in Europe', European Council on Foreign Relations website, 19 October 2016.

6. Elizabeth Braw, 'Finland's mysterious nuclear investor', *Politico*, Europe edition, 13 July 2015.

7. Vedran Pavlic, 'Media Reports: HDZ paid Ifo Institute with donation from Russian sources', *Total Croatia News*, 12 July 2016.

8. The full text of Putin's speech is available via the *Washington Post* at http://www.washingtonpost.com/wp-dyn/content/article/2007/02/12/AR2007021200555.html (accessed 16 January 2018).

9. Stacy Meichtry, Noemie Bisserbe and Matthew Dalton, 'Paris Attacks' Alleged Ringleader, Now Dead, Had Slipped Into Europe Unchecked', *Wall Street Journal*, 19 November 2015.

10. I have pieced the story of Abaaoud together from a number of sources, including 'What the Paris attacks tell us about IS strategy', *Spiegel Online*, 27 November 2015; and David A. Graham, 'The mysterious life and death of Abdelhamid Abaaoud', *The Atlantic*, 19 November 2015.

11. Details of the Pew study data are quoted in Bruce Stokes, 'The immigration crisis is tearing Europe apart', *Foreign Policy*, 22 July 2016.

Chapter 2: The Economic Storm

12. These stories and others have been told in countless newspaper articles but they are pulled together well in Gavin Hewitt, *The Lost Continent: Europe's Darkest Hour since World War Two* (London: Hodder & Stoughton, 2013).

13. Jean Pisani-Ferry et al., *Coming of Age: Report on the Euro Area*, Bruegel Blueprint 4, 2008, available at http://bruegel.org/wp-content/uploads/imported/publications/BP2008bruegel_comingofage.pdf (accessed 16 January 2018).

14. See Hewitt, *The Lost Continent*, Chapter 3; Martin Sandbu, *Europe's Orphan: The Future of the Euro and the Politics of Debt* (Princeton: Princeton University Press, 2015), Chapter 3.

15. For a more detailed discussion of what became known in Germany as the 'Hartz plan' and its effects, see Sandbu, *Europe's Orphan*, particularly Chapter 2.

16. For an account of some of the more absurd aspects of these bubbles, including the building of airports from which no planes have ever flown, see Hewitt, *The Lost Continent*, Chapter 2.

17. For a fuller discussion of this, see Sandbu, *Europe's Orphan*, pp. 33–5.

18. For an account of the approach taken with AIB see Sandbu, *Europe's Orphan*, p. 96.

19. See Graeme Wearden, 'Ireland's debt crisis: today as it happened', *The Guardian*, 18 November 2010. For an account of Honohan's conversation with Brian Lenihan mentioned lower down the page, see Sandbu, *Europe's Orphan*, pp. 80–81.

20. Michel Rose, 'Trichet's letter to Rome published, urges cuts', Reuters, 29 September 2011.

21. I draw heavily in this section on parts of Sandbu, *Europe's Orphan*, especially Chapters 4 and 7.

22. See 'How did Iceland clean up its banks?', BBC News, 10 February 2016.

23. Anna Molin, 'Denmark seizes Amagerbanken', *Wall Street Journal*, 7 February 2011.

24. On the protests in Cyprus, see Carlo Davis, 'Cypriot bail-out protests: Cypriots march against bank deal', *Huffington Post*, US edition, 18 March 2013.

25. For a discussion of the difference between the first and second deals offered to Cyprus, the stance taken up in the negotiations by the Cypriot government and the ultimate reinstatement of protections for those with less than €100,000 in savings, see 'The Cyprus bail-out: a better deal, but still painful', *The Economist*, 25 March 2013.

Chapter 3: Social Pain, Political Consequence

26. Colm McCarthy, 'Populism is flowing into Irish mainstream', Independent.ie, 12 March 2017.

27. See James Bessen, 'The automation paradox', *The Atlantic*, 19 January 2016.

28. Steve Richards, *The Rise of the Outsiders: How Mainstream Politics Lost Its Way* (London: Atlantic, 2017).

29. I have drawn Marek's story from *The European Crisis and its Human Cost: A Call for Fair Alternatives and Solutions*, Caritas Monitoring Report 2014. Caritas deserves enormous credit for not only drawing attention to the scale of the

social pain caused by the economic crisis, but for painting a vivid picture of how that crisis has affected the lives of real individuals and families.

30. See William Schomberg and David Milliken, 'Bank of England's Carney warns of strains from globalization', Reuters, 5 December 2016.

31. Ian Kearns and Denitsa Raynova, *The Foreign and Security Policies of Populist Parties in Europe: An ELN Quick Guide*, European Leadership Network, May 2014.

Chapter 4: Brexit

32. On the warnings, see for example Charlie Cooper, 'EU referendum: UK's top economic experts issue joint warning against Brexit', *The Independent*, 21 June 2016; Alex Barker et al., 'Four EU leaders warn UK voters of exit downsides', *Financial Times*, 2 June 2016.

33. One of the most incisive attacks on Cameron came on the very day the referendum vote was lost, and it came from his previous coalition partner in government, and former deputy Prime Minister, Nick Clegg. In a powerful and passionate piece of commentary, he made clear he had repeatedly refused to go along with the idea of a referendum on Brexit while in government, because 'elevating internal party rows to a national plebiscite is not good enough'. See Nick Clegg, 'Brexit: Cameron and Osborne are to blame for this sorry pass', *Financial Times*, 24 June 2016.

34. For an example of the kind of attack launched on Johnson after the referendum result became clear, see Nick Cohen, 'There are liars and then there's Boris Johnson and Michael Gove', *The Guardian*, 25 June 2016.

35. Philip Hammond was one of those making the argument against Blair. A few months after the referendum, he travelled to Davos to tell the audience of elite business leaders, politicians and policymakers there that anti-immigrant sentiment in Britain could be traced back to Blair's tenure and especially to his 'open door' policy when eight eastern European countries joined the EU in 2004. See Larry Elliott, 'Philip Hammond blames Tony Blair for Brexit vote', *The Guardian*, 20 January 2017.

36. So bad was Corbyn's performance thought to be in the campaign that it ultimately triggered a further attempt to remove him as party leader. The attack against him also highlighted a further policy fissure within the Labour Party. Corbyn was accused in particular of ignoring the concerns of many northern voters about immigration. See for example 'The Labour Party and Brexit: the culpability of Jeremy Corbyn', *The Economist*, 24 June 2016.

37. That Cameron seems to have been certain of success is one criticism made of him by Nick Clegg. Interestingly, however, since his departure from government, the former Chancellor George Osborne has made clear that he was much less sure than Cameron of the prospects of victory right from the off. See for example Tom Parfitt, 'George Osborne warned David Cameron NOT to hold EU referendum', *Daily Express*, 29 June 2016.

38. Blair himself acknowledged a link in an interview given to CNN, in which he offered what *The Guardian* later called a 'partial apology' for the Iraq war. See Martin Chulov, 'Tony Blair is right: without the Iraq war there would be no Islamic State', *The Guardian*, 25 October 2015.

39. For one of the very best accounts of the rise of UKIP, see Robert Ford and Matthew Goodwin, *Revolt on the Right: Explaining Support for the Radical Right in Britain* (Abingdon: Routledge, 2014).

40. Cameron made clear he wanted legislation to achieve this, saying: 'Never again should it be possible for a British government to transfer power to the European Union without the say of the British people in a referendum.' See 'EU Lisbon Treaty: David Cameron promises vote on future EU changes', *Daily Telegraph*, 4 November 2009.

41. For a time, No. 10 tried to portray this as Cameron doing a Thatcher, standing alone against Brussels and vetoing unacceptable EU behaviour. In reality, the rest of the members of both the euro and the EU just went ahead without the UK and agreed the new arrangements anyway. See 'David Cameron blocks EU-wide deal to tackle euro crisis', BBC News, 9 December 2011.

42. The full text of the speech can be accessed in a number of places. It was reproduced by *The Independent* on the day of Cameron's resignation and the headline said everything: see Oliver Wright and Charlie Cooper, 'The speech that was the start of the end for David Cameron', *The Independent*, 24 June 2016.

43 This sentence itself contains an interesting admission, namely that the very size of the EU's internal market is one of the biggest strengths European countries have when it comes to negotiating access to the markets of others. A point apparently not lost on Cameron, but to which the Brexiteers in his own party remain deaf.

44. For the full negotiating stance as he set it out for public consumption, see David Cameron, 'The EU is not working and we will change it', *Daily Telegraph*, 15 March 2014.

45. The full text of Cameron's speech, in which this sentence sits in a wider-ranging passage on Europe, a passage that it has to be said smacks more than a little of Euroscepticism, is available on the Conservative Party website at http://press.conservatives.com/post/98882674910/david-cameron-speech-to-conservative-party (accessed 18 January 2018).

46. The full text of this speech is available on the Gov.uk website at https://www.gov.uk/government/speeches/jcb-staffordshire-prime-ministers-speech (accessed 18 January 2018).

47. These differences, and a flavour of how they impacted on Cameron's public position, are discussed in Tim Shipman, *All Out War: The Full Story of How Brexit Sank Britain's Political Class* (London: William Collins, 2016).

48. See 'EU reform deal: what Cameron wanted and what he got', BBC News, 20 February 2016.

49. Nicholas Watt, 'Cameron told he has two weeks to persuade Poles and allies over EU', *The Guardian*, 1 February 2016.

50 Tim Shipman, *All Out War*, particularly Chapter 6, 'Guerilla Warfare'.

51. Private conversations between the author and some of the leading members of the Remain campaign team.

52. 'Alan Johnson launches Labour's "keep UK in the EU" campaign', BBC News, 1 December 2015.

53. On Obama's intervention, see Heather Stewart and Nadia Khomami, 'Barack Obama issues Brexit trade warning', *The Guardian*, 25 April 2016.

54. Denis MacShane, *Brexit: How Britain Left Europe* (London: I. B. Tauris, 2016).

55.　Paul Waugh 'Jeremy Corbyn refuses to rule out campaigning for Britain to quit the European Union', *Huffington Post*, UK edition, 25 July 2015.

56.　Quoted in MacShane, *Brexit*, p.72. The full text of the Bruges speech is available on the Margaret Thatcher Foundation website at https://www.margaret-thatcher.org/document/107332 (accessed 18 January 2018).

57.　Cameron's pledge to get immigration down to under 100,000 was always nonsense. It wasn't agreed with business or the public services and wasn't based on any assessment of what the country's needs were. That there was no serious plan developed to deliver it just rammed home the point that it was mere populist posturing.

Chapter 5: Crisis Management

58.　For the text of Draghi's comments that many credit with saving the euro, see 'Verbatim of the remarks made by Mario Draghi', ECB website, 26 July 2012, https://www.ecb.europa.eu/press/key/date/2012/html/sp120726.en.html (accessed 18 January 2018).

59.　For an overview of how efforts to strengthen the euro were proceeding as at late 2017, see Grégory Claeys, 'How to Build a Resilient Monetary Union? Lessons from the Euro Crisis', Working Paper 778, Asian Development Bank Institute, September 2017.

60.　Claire Jones and Jim Brunsden, 'ECB confirms two struggling Italian banks will close', *Financial Times*, 24 June 2017.

61.　Jim Brunsden, 'Germany stands firm against EU bank deposit guarantee plan', *Financial Times*, 11 October 2017.

62.　See Claeys, 'How to Build a Resilient Monetary Union?', p. 19.

63.　A short, translated video clip of some his visionary speech is available on the *Express* website at http://www.express.co.uk/news/world/858987/Emmanuel-Macron-Paris-France-Sorbonne-EU-speech-Angela-Merkel (accessed 18 January 2018). The full text in English is also available at: http://international.blogs.ouest-france.fr/archive/2017/09/29/macron-sorbonne-verbatim-europe-18583.html (accessed 2 February 2018).

64.　Details on all of these steps, and links to more detailed documents on each element of the strategy, are available on the Council of the European Union website at http://www.consilium.europa.eu/en/policies/fight-against-terrorism/foreign-fighters (accessed 18 January 2018).

65.　The details of the deal can be found in 'EU–Turkey Statement: Questions and Answers', European Commission, 19 March 2016, available at http://europa.eu/rapid/press-release_MEMO-16-963_en.htm (accessed 19 January 2018).

66.　Alissa J. Rubin and Jason Horowitz, 'European leaders look to Africa to stem migration', *New York Times*, 28 August 2017.

67.　James Crisp and Matthew Day, 'European divisions over migration brutally exposed by EU court judgement on refugee quotas', *Daily Telegraph*, 6 September 2017.

68　Ordo-liberalism refers to an approach to economic management that prioritises the role of markets, but aims to make them efficient and socially productive through effective regulation. This contrasts with the Keynesian approach that emphasises a bigger role for state spending.

69. See Wolfgang Munchau, 'The wacky economics of Germany's parallel universe', *Financial Times*, 16 November 2014.

70. Yanis Varoufakis, *And the Weak Suffer What They Must? Europe, Austerity and the Threat to Global Stability* (London: Vintage, 2017). See in particular Chapter 2 and Varoufakis's fascinating account of a common currency proposal offered to the Germans by then French economy minister, and later President, Valéry Giscard d'Estaing.

71. Pierre Briançon, '5 Fronts in the coming eurozone battle', *Politico*, Europe edition, 27 September 2017.

Chapter 6: Triggers of Disintegration

72. For a longer discussion of these recession risks see Simon Tilford, 'Is the Eurozone Really out of the Woods?', Centre for European Reform, September 2017 available at http://www.cer.eu/sites/default/files/insight_ST_22.9.17.pdf (accessed 19 January 2018).

73. 'Gordon Brown warns on financial crisis risks', BBC News, 28 September 2017.

74. Guy Chazan, 'Wolfgang Schäuble warns of debt-driven global financial crisis', *Financial Times*, 8 October 2017.

75. Gene Frieda, 'Fasten seatbelts, Europe is unsafe at any speed', *Financial Times*, 24 July 2017.

76. 'Significant Challenges for Italy: All You Need to Know about Key Issues', Danske Bank, August 2017, available at http://danskeresearch.danskebank.com/abo/ResearchItaly140817/$file/Research_Italy_140817.pdf (accessed 19 January 2018).

77. Cheyenne Ligon and Allison Fedirka, 'The evolution of Italy's banking crisis', Geopolitical Futures website, 30 December 2016.

78. For an assessment that the SRF may ultimately be enough, see Daniel Gros and Willem Pieter De Groen, 'The Single Resolution Fund: how much is needed', Vox website, 15 December 2015.

79. Pieter Cleppe, 'Win or lose, Marine Le Pen is a nightmare for the EU', CNN, 24 April 2017.

80. Nicholas Vinocur, 'French far-left firebrand's campaign of revenge', *Politico*, European edition, 31 March 2017.

81. See Romain Brunet, 'EU reform: Hamon wants a new deal, Mélenchon threatens to slam the door', France24, 13 March 2017.

82. Natalie Nougayrède, 'Anti-German, soft on Putin – Mélenchon is no saviour of the left', *The Guardian*, 18 April 2017.

83. Pierre Briançon, 'François Fillon at pains to stand apart on Europe', *Politico*, Europe edition, 8 April 2017.

84. David Chazan, 'Presidential candidate François Fillon calls for France to "ignore" Schengen and have "real" borders with Europe', *Daily Telegraph*, 24 January 2017.

85. Adam Nossiter, 'A candidate rises on vows to control Islam and immigration. This time in France', *New York Times*, 25 November 2016.

86. Tony Barber, 'Italy's centre-right draws hope from elections in Sicily', *Financial Times*, 7 November 2017.

87. 'New Five Star Movement leader: we want to stay in the EU', The Local.it, 25 September 2017.

88. Jacopo Barigazzi, 'The Italian movement that could remake Europe', *Politico*, Europe edition, 1 December 2016.
89. Giada Zampano, 'Italy's Northern League to launch campaign for EU referendum', *Wall Street Journal*, 24 June 2016.
90. Jacopo Barigazzi and Giulia Paravicini, 'Italy's Northern League goes soft (on the euro)', *Politico*. Europe edition, 24 August 2017.
91. Anna Momigliano, 'Italy's Northern League goes local to stay national', *Politico*, Europe edition, 18 October 2017.
92. Luca Romano, 'Silvio Berlusconi: "Con la doppia moneta si rilanciano i consumi"', Il Giornale.it, 20 August 2017.
93. Ambrose Evans-Pritchard, 'Spain threatens to break up the euro unless Catalonia comes to heel', *Daily Telegraph*, 28 September 2017.
94. Phillipe Legrain, 'EU membership both encourages separatism and frustrates it', *Brussels Times*, 19 October 2017.
95. Timothy Ash, 'Turkey's EU accession: the way forward', *Financial Times*, 20 September 2017.
96. 'Turkey accuses Germany and others of blackmail over EU bid', *Financial Times*, 14 September 2017.
97. Mark Leonard, 'Brave New Europe', *New York Review of Books*, 9–22 November 2017, p. 47.
98. Susi Dennison, 'The Future of Schengen', European Council on Foreign Relations, 2016.
99. Genevieve Zingg, 'The Consequences of Schengen's Collapse: Populist Shortsightedness and the Future of European Security', Institute of European Democrats, 2016, available at https://www.iedonline.eu/download/2016/schengen/ZINGG.pdf (accessed 22 January 2018).

Chapter 7: The Economy from Trigger to Collapse

100. Roger Bootle, *Leaving the euro: A practical guide* (London: Capital Economics, 2012).
101. Panicos O. Demetriades, 'Frexit: how a Le Pen victory could unleash a tsunami of economic volatility', *The Conversation*, 24 April 2017.
102. Soeren Kern, 'Could Italy bring down the euro?', Gatestone Institute, 14 July 2016.
103. Anja Ettel and Holger Zschäpitz, 'In Europa zittern wieder die Banken', *Die Welt*, 7 July 2016.
104. Wolfgang Munchau, 'Italy is key to survival of euro and the EU', *Irish Times*, 21 November 2016, available at https://www.irishtimes.com/business/economy/wolfgang-munchau-italy-is-key-to-survival-of-euro-and-eu-1.2876532 (accessed 5 February 2018).
105. Wolfgang Munchau, 'Italy may be the next domino to fall', *Financial Times*, 26 June 2016.
106 Roger Bootle, *Leaving the euro: A practical guide* (London: Capital Economics, 2012), p. 84. The specific country being referred to in the original is Greece, but the argument applies equally to other possible cases of euro exit.
107. Daniel Lacalle, 'France exiting the euro would be the largest sovereign default in history with serious contagion effects', CNBC, 22 February 2017.

108 For a discussion of this issue, see Willem Buiter, *Can Central Banks Go Broke?*, Centre for Economic Policy Research, Policy Insight No. 24, May 2008, available at https://cepr.org/sites/default/files/policy_insights/PolicyInsight24.pdf (accessed 5 February 2018).

109. Demetriades, 'Frexit'.

110 Anders Aslund, *Why a Breakup of the Euro Area Must Be Avoided: Lessons from Previous Breakups*, Peterson Institute of International Economics, Policy Brief PB12–20, August 2012, p. 4. Available at http://citeseerx.ist.psu.edu/viewdoc/download?doi=10.1.1.259.7047&rep=rep1&type=pdf (accessed 2 February 2018).

111 Mark Cliffe, *EMU Break-up: Pay Now, Pay Later*, ING Financial Markets Research, 1 December 2011 available at https://markcliffe.files.wordpress.com/2011/12/emubreakup-0112112.pdf (accessed 30 January 2018).

112. John Bruton, 'What Would Happen if the EU Broke Up?', European Policy Brief, Federal Trust, November 2012, p. 3, available at http://fedtrust.co.uk/wp-content/uploads/2014/12/Policy_Brief_John_Bruton.pdf (accessed 22 January 2018).

113. Sebastian Dullien, 'Why the Euro Crisis Threatens the European Single Market', European Council on Foreign Relations, October 2012, p.3, available at http://www.ecfr.eu/page/-/ECFR64_EU_CRISIS_MEMO_AW.pdf (accessed 22 January 2018).

Chapter 8: Politics after the European Union

114. From the Consolidated Version of the Treaty on European Union, available on the EUR-Lex website at http://eur-lex.europa.eu/legal-content/EN/TXT/?uri=celex:12012M002 (accessed 22 January 2018).

115. Liam Byrne (a member of the said committee), 'Why Juncker is wrong: the good ship Europe is sinking', *Huffington Post*, UK edition, 13 September 2017.

116. J. Lester Feder, 'March led by authoritarian group in Poland draws tens of thousands from across Europe', *BuzzFeed News*, 11 November 2017.

117. Ian Cobain and Matthew Taylor, 'Language school run by Italian fascist leader', *The Guardian*, 29 February 2008.

118. Naomi Grimley, 'Do Europe's "illiberal democrats" challenge the EU's values?', BBC News, 14 November 2017, available at http://www.bbc.co.uk/news/world-europe-41904508 (accessed 5 February 2018).

119. Heather Grabbe and Stefan Lehne, 'Defending EU values in Poland and Hungary', Carnegie Europe, 4 September 2017.

120. Quoted ibid.

121. This account of the Greek–German tensions draws on Mark Lowen, 'Debt-Laden Greeks give vent to anti-German Feelings', BBC News, 27 February 2012.

122. Jim Yardley, 'As insults fly in the Greek and German media, some wish for less news', *New York Times*, 29 May 2015.

123. All Trump quotes here taken from Glenn Kessler, 'Trump's trade rhetoric, stuck in a time warp', *Washington Post*, 18 March 2016.

124. Rositsa Kratunkova, 'Tax competition undermines European values of solidarity', *Financial Times*, 21 November 2017.

125. This and the later example from Bornheim drawn from Alexander Betts, 'The Elephant in the Room: Islam and the Crisis of Liberal Values in Europe', *Foreign Affairs*, 2 February 2016.

126. Diane Taylor, 'Asylum seekers made to wear coloured wristbands in Cardiff', *The Guardian*, 24 January 2016.

127. Ivan Krastev, *After Europe* (Philadelphia: University of Pennsylvania Press, 2017), p. 73.

128. Ivan Krastev, *After Europe* (Philadelphia: University of Pennsylvania Press, 2017), p. 79.

129. Prime Minister Viktor Orbán's press conference on 24 February 2016 in Budapest. The full text is available in English on the Hungarian government website at http://www.kormany.hu/en/the-prime-minister/the-prime-minister-s-speeches/prime-minister-viktor-orban-s-press-conference (accessed 22 January 2018).

130. Lydia Gall, 'Hungary's Xenophobic Anti-Migrant Campaign', Human Rights Watch, 13 September 2016. See also Krastev, *After Europe*, p. 102.

Chapter 9: Shattered Peace?

131. For one of the best, most readable histories of how today's Europe emerged from the ashes of 1945, see Tony Judt, *Postwar: A History of Europe since 1945* (London: Vintage, 2010).

132. The director of the European Council on Foreign Relations, Mark Leonard, famously captured some of this sentiment in his book *Why Europe Will Run the 21st Century* (London: Fourth Estate, 2005). Others were always more sceptical. See for example the review of Leonard's book by Martin Jacques, 'Two cheers for Europe', *The Guardian*, 19 March 2005.

133. The full text of the North Atlantic Treaty is available on the NATO website at https://www.nato.int/cps/en/natolive/official_texts_17120.htm (accessed 23 January 2018).

134. This debate has been going on for decades, with the principal American claim being that the US takes far too much of the burden while much of Europe, relatively speaking, freeloads under US protection. In recent years, however, and even in the Obama administration, the criticism from Washington has grown more and more stark and warnings have been issued to the effect that things can't go on as they are for much longer. It was this pressure that led to a declaration at the NATO summit in Wales in 2014 to the effect that all members of the alliance would increase their defence expenditure. Delivery since has been what diplomats might describe as patchy.

135. Marine Le Pen's approach would be an illustrative example. She favours a big increase in expenditure on a number of areas of security, including defence and prisons, an expansion of the police force, and tighter control of borders.

136. The one possible exception here would be UK–French defence collaboration. The UK and France are western Europe's two serious military powers, both possessing nuclear weapons and the capacity to project military power over distance via the use of aircraft carriers. As noted in Chapter 5 of this book, they also recently agreed to deepen defence cooperation, including on some nuclear matters, via bilateral treaties signed at Lancaster House in London

in 2010. However, this kind of defence cooperation requires the two governments to share a foreign and defence policy outlook and to be willing to act in defence of common values and interests. In a post-EU Europe, everything would depend on what sort of governments were in power in London and Paris. The days when value and outlook alignment could be assumed as a given might be over, especially if France had fallen to Eurosceptic and nationalist forces.

137. I addressed this issue in a recent piece co-authored with the Labour MP, Liam Byrne. See Liam Byrne and Ian Kearns, 'Our obsession with Brexit has blinded us to the weakening of the west', *New Statesman*, 12 September 2017.

138. James Kynge and Michael Peel, 'Brussels rattled as China reaches out to eastern Europe', *Financial Times*, 27 November 2017.

139. Ibid.

140. This formulation of the German question as a choice between a European Germany and a German Europe is drawn from Timothy Garton Ash, *In Europe's Name: Germany and the Divided Continent* (London: Vintage, 1994).

141. For an account of the Russian narrative, and its consistency over time, it is worth reading President Putin's speech to the Munich Security Conference on 10 February 2007, available on the Kremlin website at http://en.kremlin.ru/events/president/transcripts/24034, and also his speech on the annexation of Crimea, delivered in Moscow on 18 March 2014, available at http://en.kremlin.ru/events/president/news/20603 (both accessed 23 January 2018).

142. For a fuller account of the competing Russian and Western narratives and for a report on a discussion of them involving analysts from both Russia and the West see Thomas Frear and Lukasz Kulesa (eds), 'Competing Western and Russian Narratives on European Order: Is There Common Ground?', European Leadership Network and Russian International Affairs Council, April 2016, available at https://www.europeanleadershipnetwork.org/wp-content/uploads/2017/10/ELN-Competing-Narratives-Report.pdf (accessed 23 January 2018).

143. For a discussion of this see Roy Allison, *Russia, the West, and Military Intervention* (Oxford: Oxford University Press, 2013).

144. Despite this the end of the Cold War, when it came, was a roller-coaster ride the like of which no one ought ever to try to repeat. And it was only afterwards that it became clear how close the world had come to destruction on a number of occasions. For a superb account of some of the scarier moments embedded in that history, and an account of how the confrontation ended, see David E. Hoffman, *The Dead Hand: Reagan, Gorbachev and the Untold Story of the Cold War Arms Race* (London: Icon, 2011).

145. To my mind, this is one of the key lessons from nineteenth- and twentieth-century Europe. A brilliant, rich analysis of some of the challenges and difficulties of managing a balance of power can be found in A. J. P. Taylor, *The Struggle for Mastery in Europe 1848–1918* (Oxford: Oxford University Press, 1954).

146. Winston Churchill, 'Their Finest Hour' speech to the House of Commons, 18 June 1940. Transcript at Hansard, HC Deb, vol. 362, col. 61.